Surviving The New Boss

IONA ROSE

Author's Note

Hey there!

Thank you for choosing my book. I sure hope that you love it. I'd hate to part ways once you're done though. So how about we stay in touch?

My newsletter is a great way to discover more about me and my books. Where you'll find frequent exclusive giveaways, sneak previews of new releases and be first to see new cover reveals.

And as a HUGE thank you for joining, you'll receive a FREE book on me!

With love,

Iona

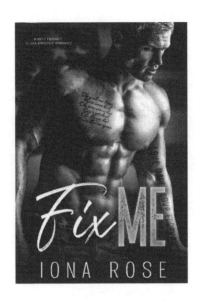

Get Your FREE Book Here:
https://dl.bookfunnel.com/v9yit8b3f7

Prologue
ALEX

I cast a critical eye over my grandfather as he sits back in his favorite chair. People are always saying he looks good for a man in his early eighties, and the truth is, he looks good for a man twenty years younger than that. That doesn't stop me from worrying about him though, especially not when he has summoned me so formally in the middle of the work week.

My grandfather is by far the most important person in my life. My grandmother died of pneumonia before I was born, and my parents were killed in an accident when I was four years old. My grandfather took me in and raised me and the thought of losing him is more than I can bear.

"Are you done?" my grandfather asks.

I frown at him. I have no idea what he's talking about.

Quite suddenly, his stern-looking face breaks into a smile and his blue eyes sparkle. There may be lines around his eyes, but they are as sharp as ever. Even his graying hair doesn't make him look old. If I look half as good as he does now when I'm his age, I'll be truly happy. "You've been checking me over, trying to see if you can work out what I'm dying from."

"Grandad," I exclaim. "I was not."

"Promise me something Alex," my grandfather says, his expression serious and I nod. His expression changes instantly and he grins as he continues. "Never play poker because your poker face is the worst one I've ever seen."

I can't help but laugh and hold my hands up in mock surrender.

"Ok. You got me," I say. "I'll admit I was concerned that you wanted to see me so urgently in the middle of the day when we should both be at work."

"There is a reason for that. And it's nothing to do with my health or longevity. I requested your presence during working hours because this is about business."

Now that I've recovered from my initial panic about his health, my curiosity is more than piqued. My grandfather is the owner and CEO of Waters Financial, a company he built from the ground up into a billion-dollar endeavor. I currently work as a manager in a small marketing agency. I can't see any reason why my grandfather would need a business meeting with me. It's not like he's going to hire the company I work for and vice versa because we agreed a long time ago that we wouldn't ever consider doing that. We wouldn't muddy the waters by working together like that.

I know one day I will take over Waters Financial. Not just one day. In three years to be precise, when my grandfather turns eighty-five. In the meantime, it was decided that rather than working at the firm, I should work in other places to learn my own style of management and get some experience in the world of business and without the safety net of knowing my grandfather owned the company. I liked the idea because it meant I got to make my mistakes away from my grandfather's watchful eye, and also because I don't think it's easy for staff to see you as their boss when you've been their friend working on the same level as them.

I went to college and studied business and management and then I did a bunch of other courses on the finance side of business at night school while I worked my way up the ranks to a manager in the company I work for.

"I want to know how you would feel about bringing the timeline for my retirement forward," my grandfather says. "I'm thinking next month if that gives you enough time to work out your notice period at your current job. Assuming you want to bring this forward of course."

My head is spinning. I was right; he is ill. He has to be. He would never choose to retire this early if he wasn't. Hell, I even had a hard time getting him to agree to retire at eighty-five. Left to his own devices he would have happily worked until he dropped dead at his desk and even then, I could imagine his ghost standing impatiently in the corner dishing out the orders.

"You're making that face again," my grandfather remarks. "The one where you're planning my funeral in the back of your mind."

"Stop it," I scold, my voice a bit harsher than I had meant it to be. "It's not funny Grandad. Tell me what's going on with your health."

"I'm sorry," my grandfather says. "I shouldn't have teased you. But I told you I'm fine and I am. I... God this sounds crazy at my age... but I've met someone. Someone I'd like to spend my last years with, and I don't want to wait another three years for that to start."

For a moment, I'm so stunned I can't speak and then it hits me. He was in love! And I grin at him. It's about bloody time he found happiness outside of the office.

"You old dog," I say with a laugh.

"Hey, less of the old," my grandfather says, also laughing.

His laughter fades and he looks at me seriously once more. "So, is bringing the timeline of me retiring and you taking over running Waters Financial forward something you are willing to do, or at least consider?"

"Yes, of course," I say without hesitation.

Career-wise, I feel like I'm more than ready to do this, and on a personal level, I want nothing more than for my grandfather to be happy. "I'm happy to take over now and have you live your life outside of work. But we'll hash out the details of all of that in a minute. First, I want to know everything about the woman who managed the miracle of taming the self-proclaimed bachelor Evan Waters."

Grandpa's face softens. "Her name is Irene. Irene Randall. She's eighty years old and she's a widow too. She lost her husband ten years ago. We met at a book club, and we got to talking and found out that we had quite a lot in common and well, the rest is history as the saying goes," my grandfather says, smiling the whole time.

"She must be quite a woman," I say.

"Oh, she is," he replies.

"When do I get to meet her?" I ask.

"Soon. Now enough with the gossip. Let's get down to business. The first and perhaps most important thing – Waters Financial will be your company and you can run it however you see fit, with one exception. I want it written into the handover contract that you can't replace any of the staff for the first year. Obviously, there will be exceptions. If someone is under performing or whatever, but some of those guys have been with me for ten to twenty years, and are like family to me. I won't have you go in and bulldozer them all out."

"What makes you think I would do that?" I ask.

"Because you represent change," he says. "Management style in my day was about the employer looking out for their staff and being rewarded for that with loyalty. Now it's more important to slim down the staff bill and fuck the fact that means Henry's kids are going to starve to death and Darlene will never get that vacation she's been saving for the last two years for."

"I wouldn't want anyone's kids to starve or Darlene to miss out on her dream holiday, but I take your point. However, as I have said to you many times, I do think the company is overstaffed."

There is no point in lying about it. I've said it often enough.

"I know you do. Hence the clause. I am hopeful that by the end of a year, you see it works perfectly well without culling anyone, and if not, well I think most of the staff know your thoughts on the subject, and a year should be long enough for them to make other arrangements," my grandfather says.

"Ok," I agree. I had a feeling my grandfather would put some sort of clause in about the staff and I knew there was no point in fighting him on it because they were like a second family to him. I could probably get some wiggle room, but I didn't want to dig my heels in and risk my grandfather calling the whole thing off and missing out on his early retirement.

"What else?" I ask.

"That's about it, to be honest. I trust you to make good decisions and make me proud," he says. "And as for the day-to-day running of the business, I don't think it will look good if you come in and shadow me. I think the staff will just see you as my grandson that way. I will introduce you to Ros, my assistant, well your assistant now, and she can show you the ropes rather than me."

"I already have an assistant. I'll be bringing Celia over with me," I say. "But it will be nice to have someone show me the ropes and then we can find her another role in the company once I'm settled in."

My grandfather is shaking his head before I even finish talking.

"No," he says. "I'm sorry son, but Ros is going to be your assistant. She's worked for me for three years and she's the best assistant I have ever had. She doesn't take nonsense, which is definitely a skill she'll need with you." He pauses and smiles to soften the blow a little bit, but I can see that he has made his mind up.

"But I already promised Celia," I say.

"Well, that was rather foolish, and a good lesson. Never promise something to someone that isn't yours to give away," he says.

I must look as pissed off as I feel because he relents a little bit.

"Look I'm not saying don't give her a job. She must be good if you want to bring her with you. But it won't be as your personal assistant role. There is actually an opening for a receptionist for the main desk on the management floor. I was going to hire someone before I left, but if you want the role for Celia say it now and it's hers."

I think about it. Celia isn't going to be all that happy about being chucked on reception, and I'm not exactly happy about it myself, but if she's at the company, I can weasel my way around having her do bits of the assistant's job that I don't trust a stranger with.

"Yes, I'll give her that role," I say.

"Is there anyone else you're planning on bringing over with you?" Grandpa asks.

"Just Will," I say. "Ideally I'd like him to be head of security, but don't worry, I'll continue paying his salary personally."

"Alex, Will isn't qualified to be head of security," my grandfather says.

"Are you kidding me? It was you that found him for me and you told me he was one of the best."

I hired Will nine years ago after someone tried to kidnap me for ransom, and he has been my personal bodyguard ever since. I'm shocked to find out that after recommending him, my grandfather doesn't actually think he's any good.

"Calm down," my grandfather says. "Will is the best at what he does. But unless he's been to university without me knowing it since you hired him, he isn't qualified to run an IT department."

"Ok, back up there. Why on earth would I want him to work in the IT department?" I ask.

"I don't know," my grandfather says. "But you just said you want him to run it."

"Oh no," I say as understanding dawns on me. "I don't mean cybersecurity. I mean actual physical security. He will mostly still be my personal bodyguard, but he can liaise with your current security team and help strengthen them."

"Ah," my grandfather says. "Well, that makes more sense. But, well, we don't actually have a security department."

"Even after I was almost kidnapped?" I ask.

My grandfather nods. "No one wants to kidnap me. You were the target, and you are now safe," he says. "But by all means bring Will on board. I assumed you would. And if you and he think that there is a need for more security, as I said, you are free to run the company how you see fit."

Except for whom I get to have as my personal assistant apparently, I think, but don't say. Instead, I smile at my grandfather.

"Thank you," I say. "I'll definitely feel better having Will around."

We iron out a few more points and it soon becomes clear that we are mostly on the same page with everything regarding the business. The only issue I have with the way my grandfather runs Waters Financial is the overstaffing issue and he has already made sure that is covered in a way I can't affect for at least a year.

Because of how similar my grandfather and I are, I guess it makes sense that we mostly see things the same way, and I think that it's for that reason that it's not long before we both agree that the thick of the negotiations are taken care of, and my grandfather goes and makes us some tea and sandwiches and we enjoy lunch together.

We chat about Irene some more and I discover that my grandfather wants to take her traveling around Europe and Asia. I almost warn him to be careful that she's not just after his money, but my grandfather is no fool and it's not like she's some twenty-year-old bimbo. I bite my tongue and just enjoy his happiness instead. So what if she's after his money. If she can make him smile like that... good luck to her. And it's not like he doesn't have more than enough to spoil her rotten without it even making a dent in his bank account. And I know he's not stupid enough to get married without an ironclad prenuptial agreement in place first.

After lunch, I say my goodbyes, get back in my car and head back to the office. Will is driving and I tell him about the meeting I've just had with my grandfather and officially give him the offer to move over with me. I explain that he would still chiefly be working for me, but that he would also be dealing with security at the company.

He's cool with this as I knew he would be.

I have two tasks to do when I get back to the office. Neither of them is going to be as easy as telling Will about the changes. The first of the tasks, I don't mind which is writing my resignation letter, and the second one, I'm already dreading, which is telling Celia she's going to be a receptionist and not my personal assistant assuming she still wants to move over with me. She is not going to take that news well and I feel bad for having to let her down, but that's the way it is, and I'd rather tell her and get it over with today.

Once I'm in my office, with Will stationed outside of my door as always, I type out and send my resignation letter and then I call Celia into my office. She stands before me, staring down at me. I always forget how tall Celia is until I'm seated and she's standing. She's not uncomfortably tall; her willowy frame somehow suits her height. Her feline-shaped eyes and red bob give her an almost cat-like appearance that suggests grace, which she oozes. She is always immaculately dressed and today is no different. She's wearing a simple black, knee length dress and black boots and this only adds to her feline illusion.

"Who died?" she asks.

"Huh?" I grunt.

"You disappear on a secret family matter and come back and call me in here and then don't speak. Something bad must have happened."

I decide to try and put a positive spin on this. After all, Celia is my employee and it's not my job to make her happy, but I did promise her the position and I hate to go back on my word.

"No one died," I say. "In fact, it was good news."

Celia sits down and whistles through her teeth.

"If this is your happy face, I'd hate to see you after getting bad news," she says.

"I went to have lunch with my grandfather," I explain. "And it turns out he would like to retire earlier than originally planned. Earlier, as in next month."

Celia raises an eyebrow at this.

"One of the clauses I have to agree to in order to take over the company is that the current staff members need to stay in place for at least one year."

"But you always say the company is massively overstaffed," she points out.

"I know, and believe me, I still think that. But it's better to run less productively for a year and then clean things up than not get the chance to turn things around at all."

Celia considers this and nods in agreement.

"Obviously that means I have to retain my grandfather's current personal assistant."

"Wait," Celia snaps, her neutral expression turns to one of betrayal. "Are you saying you're not taking me with you after you promised to?"

"No, of course not," I say.

Celia relaxes slightly, although she still looks wary.

I suppose, thinking of what I'm about to drop on her, she has a right to be. "You are still coming with me. But to start with, you'll be working on the management's main reception team until I find a perfectly good reason that my grandfather can't argue with to get rid of the current assistant."

"I'm not a receptionist Alex," Celia mutters. "I could walk into any personal assistant role in any company, and you know it, but I chose to be loyal to you. And this is how you repay me?"

I can feel myself getting annoyed now. I knew she wasn't going to be happy about the change, but my hands are tied. I have no choice and she needs to get onboard before I lose my patience altogether.

"Yes, how awful of me to give you an easier role for the same pay and bonuses while you bide your time to get your original job back," I say sarcastically.

"Ok, that's slightly better," Celia says. She sighs. "But a receptionist? Really?"

"Unless you've got an accountancy degree that I don't know about, then yes, a receptionist," I say.

"Fine," Celia huffs. "But I can't wait a year. I'll get the bitch fired myself if I have to."

"Please don't do anything stupid. Let's just make the move and get settled in first," I say.

"Ok, whatever," Celia says. "Well, I guess I'd best go and write my resignation letter."

She stands up and heads toward the door of my office. As she goes, I can hear her muttering under her breath; "Me, a fucking receptionist. Fuck that for a lark."

I wait until she's opening the door.

"Suck it up, buttercup," I say.

She turns around and gives me the finger, then closes the door behind her.

"You'd best be on high alert because I am this close to killing him myself," I hear Celia saying to Will and I picture her holding up her thumb and her finger, a small gap between them.

I laugh and shake my head. A death threat was the least I expected to be honest, so all in all, that went pretty well, I think.

CHAPTER
One

ROS

I'm feeling a little bit nervous as I head into work today. I don't know why. Well, no, actually, that's a lie. I do know why I'm nervous - it's because I'm going to be meeting my new boss this morning. But I don't really think that's a bad thing and I shouldn't be nervous about it, although telling myself that does absolutely nothing to stop me from being nervous.

Mr. Waters is the best boss and I absolutely adore him, and I can't imagine his grandson being anything but nice and a real gentleman because Mr. Waters raised him for the most part. I don't suppose he'll be as loved as his grandfather because those are some mighty big shoes to fill, but I'm sure we'll all get along just fine, and my nerves will be gone within five minutes of meeting him. It's not like it's some hot shot manager type coming in off the streets, someone who is bound to ruffle feathers. I think Mr. Waters' grandson will want to come in and have things run smoothly, if for no other reason than to prove to his grandfather that he is up to the task.

Friday was Mr. Waters' last official day, and we spent the

day going through everything and making sure every bit of paperwork was in order, every client was happy, and every project was on track. Today is Monday, and Mr. Waters is coming in at ten o'clock to give me a chance to set up for the morning first and deal with anything urgent before he gets here, and then he's going to introduce me to his grandson. There will be a quick company meeting to introduce the new boss to everyone else and then Mr. Waters will be gone forever, and it will be on me to get the new Mr. Waters up to speed with everything. No pressure on me there then.

I'm determined not to cry when it's time for Mr. Waters to leave. Then again, I was determined not to cry at his surprise goodbye party on Friday afternoon too, but I still did. This is different though. That was a party, a social event, and this is business and I know I need to remain professional. I don't want the new boss to think I'm one of those women who spends half her day in the bathroom crying. At least at the party I was far from the only one who shed a few tears.

I go into the building. It is four floors and Mr. Waters and I work on the fourth floor. I get into the elevator and hit the button that will take me up there. I get out of the elevator on my floor and look both ways along the corridor it opens out onto. There is no sign of life along my corridor which makes sense because I know I'm the first one here. Along the other side, there are people already in and working. From the reception desk on our floor, visitors can go to their left or to their right. Left takes them to the offices of most of the department heads, the vice president of the company and the CFO. Right takes them to the CEO and me.

Of course, the reception desk opposite the elevator is manned, as it is from seven am through to eight pm, Monday to Friday. I exchange good mornings and a bit of small talk with the ladies at the reception desk as I do every morning, and then I turn right and head to my desk. I like the set-up of where my desk is situated in relation to Mr. Waters' office.

The lower three floors of the building are pretty much all glass walls. Everyone can see everyone, and the partitions are mostly about noise reduction so people can make calls and concentrate on their work easier. I hate that setup. I have nothing to hide, but that doesn't mean I want to be on display in a glass bowl. And when I think of the set ups downstairs where the assistant's desks face the office of the person they work for, it makes me shudder. Talk about awkward. Luckily for me, Mr. Waters feels the same way about the glass, and he refused to have his office on show.

His is tucked down at the end of the corridor and it has actual walls. My little annex is in front of the office, and I face away from the door when I'm sitting at my desk with a wall behind me. There is a gap to my side for people to walk through and myself and Mr. Waters are the only people who work along here, so anyone who comes along here is usually going straight to the office anyway, because unless Mr. Waters is expecting them, it's unlikely they'll get through the main reception and the reception of the fourth floor. If that does happen, I'm the last line of defense. Only once has it almost gotten ugly. A pissed off client was yelling at me when I refused to let him see Mr. Waters without an appointment, but Mr. Waters heard the commotion and came out of his office. He made the client apologize to me before he would even entertain hearing him out. That is something else I really like about Mr. Waters. He keeps his clients happy, but never at the expense of his staff. It is always made clear that we are to be treated respectfully.

I reach my desk and hang my jacket on the back of my chair and put my purse under my desk. I sit down and hit play on the voicemails on my desk phone while I open my emails on my computer. I make a few notes of people I need to call back, but there's nothing urgent so I turn my attention to my emails. Again, there's nothing urgent so I start working through them from the top down just for something to do while I wait for Mr. Waters and his grandson to arrive.

I've replied to all the emails and returned nearly all of the calls when I spot Mr. Waters coming along the corridor. I am surprised to see that he's alone. Has everything changed? Is Mr. Waters staying on here after all? I hope so but I doubt it's anything that big.

"Good morning, Ros," he says with a wide smile as he reaches my desk.

"Good morning, Mr. Waters," I say.

I want to ask why he is alone, but I can't think of a polite way to word the question. I'm saved from asking by Mr. Waters himself.

"Is Alex here yet?" he asks.

"No," I say.

"He shouldn't be much longer then. Come on into my office so you can meet him," he says.

I dutifully get up and follow Mr. Waters into his office. I don't know why I assumed the two of them would arrive together, but it seems I got that bit wrong. We barely get seated when the door opens and in walks the most beautiful man I have ever seen in my life.

The first thing I notice is his eyes. There are neither brown nor green, but somewhere in between. His gaze is cool and intense and even behind his black framed glasses, I can see his eyelashes are longer than they have a right to be. His nose is perfectly straight and just right for his face and his lips are just right for kissing – not too big, and not too small. He has black hair which he's wearing slightly long on top and short around the sides. He's tall and even though he's wearing a suit, including the jacket, I can see the definition of his body beneath it. He definitely works out.

"Ros, this is Alex Waters, my grandson and the new CEO of Waters Financial. Alex, this is Rosalie Thomas, your assistant, the company expert, and your lifesaver in general," Mr. Waters says.

I get up as he's speaking and smile at Alex. He doesn't smile back at me, and I see that where Mr. Waters' eyes are warm, Alex's are cold. And now I'm no longer dazzled by the unexpected beauty of him, I can see that the way he holds his chin slightly too high makes him look arrogant and haughty.

"Well, that's some description to live up to," Alex says, shaking my outstretched hand. He still doesn't smile, and he drops my hand the second it's appropriate to.

I realize I'm glad he is no longer touching my hand. Pretty or not, I have taken an instant dislike to this guy and judging by the way he's looking me up and down, he feels exactly the same way about me.

"Yes," I reply. "Think yourself lucky that all you need to live up to your introduction is the right DNA."

Alex glares at me and I wonder if I have overstepped the mark when he starts to open his mouth to say something back, but Mr. Waters stops him from snapping at me by throwing his head back and laughing.

"And did I mention she's funny," he says.

"Oh, now you're making me blush," I say and ignoring Alex's butt hurt expression, I join Mr. Waters' in his laughter.

Mr. Waters checks the time.

"The department heads should all be gathered in the conference room now," he says. "This won't take long, and it doesn't need any minutes taken. Why don't you make us a drink Ros, and we'll be back in five minutes."

I nod.

"The usual?" I say and Mr. Waters nods his head. I turn toward his grandson. "What would you like to drink, Mr. Waters?"

"Coffee with cream and one sugar please," he says. "And call me Alex. I don't like all this 'Mr. Waters' shit."

"Alex," Mr. Waters chastises him.

"What?" he says. "You know I think it's too formal."

"I don't mean that, I mean using that kind of language to a lady," Mr. Waters says.

They are heading out as they speak and I'm behind them, ready to head to the little break area at our side of the corridor. As I turn off, I hear Alex's reply.

"She's going to have to get a thicker skin if that offends her," he says.

I don't hear Mr. Waters reply and I smile to myself. Alex is going to be very surprised about how thick my skin is. I have never objected to cussing; Mr. Waters is just an old school gentleman who chooses not to use that language in front of women.

I can already see Alex is going to be trouble, but hopefully it's just until he settles in, like the new lion nipping at the pack until they forget their old boss and answer only to him. If Alex is a lion, I'll be a tiger. I'm not going to let him intimidate me. I learned that I am worth more than some guy's derision early on in my adult life and I don't intend to sit back and have Alex demean me. He doesn't have to like me, but he does have to respect me or at the very least pretend to convincingly enough that I can't tell the difference.

I reach the break area, which is at the end of Mr. Waters' office, behind my desk area. There's a kitchen that Mr. Waters and I also use as a break room. It has a large fridge that's always fully stocked with sodas and water and various sandwiches and snacks. There are cakes, cookies, chips and all kinds of things in the cupboards too, plus fresh fruit is brought in every day and some days, there are pastries brought in too. Every break room has the same setup although I figure it's likely something Alex will cut, especially along here where there is only two of us and the majority of the food stuff goes to the food bank at the end of each day.

There is also a gent's bathroom and a lady's bathroom. I love it because it is essentially my own private bathroom except for the odd time a female client who is visiting Mr. Waters in his office needs to use it, so it's never dirty or gross.

I make three cups of coffee - Alex's with cream and one sugar, Mr. Waters's with no cream and two sugars, and mine with cream but no sugar. It's funny how the same drink can be made in so many different ways I think to myself as I carry the coffees back to Mr. Waters' office to wait for him and Alex to return. I suppose I had best start thinking of the office as Alex's office now. It doesn't feel right, but I'm sure it will in time.

While I wait, the phone rings and I take the call from Mr. Waters' (sorry, Alex's) desk. I take the caller's name and number and a brief description of what they want. I jot it down on a piece of paper and place it into the tray like I have a thousand times. It's the first time I've seen the in-tray empty except for the one message. Mr. Waters did a good job of tying up all his loose ends on Friday.

It's not long before the two men return.

"How did it go?" I ask Alex, trying to make conversation with him. I'm hoping I'm wrong about him and he's just a bit shy or a bit overwhelmed. It'll be so much easier for us both if we can get along.

"Fine," Alex says. "There isn't much that can go wrong with a meet and greet."

"True enough," I say, annoyed but refusing to show it.

"Oh, look Alex. Your first message," Mr. Waters says, nodding toward the in-tray.

Alex picks up the piece of paper and looks at me.

"Is this some sort of hazing?" he asks.

"Huh?" I ask.

Not my most professional response granted but he caught me by surprise, and I have no idea what he's talking about.

"A phone message scribbled on a piece of paper?" he says. "You can't seriously think that's ok."

I want to tell him it's been ok for the whole time I've been here and if he doesn't like it to shove it up his ass, but again, Mr. Waters comes to my rescue before I can say anything that can get me fired.

"It's the way we've always done it, Alex. Don't have a go at Ros for following my directions," he says.

Alex rolls his eyes.

"I should have known," he says. "Mr. Old Fashioned there. Rosalie, do some research and find an electronic message system that integrates with our schedules and whatnot and get the best one to suit our needs."

"Will do," I say. "And please, call me Ros. I only get called Rosalie when I'm in trouble."

"Then you'd best not make a mess of your first task," he replies with a tightly lined lip that I think is meant to be a smile.

"I think I can handle it," I say. "And don't worry. Once I purchase and install it, I'll even show you how to work it."

I know I shouldn't have said that, but I did, and I'm pleased I did because if he calls me out on it, I can play innocent and say I was being helpful. But we both know I wasn't.

"How... kind," he says, filling in the word 'kind' after a pause that lets me know that's not the word that he wanted to use any more than I wanted to be helpful.

I hate that I like the idea of the new system Alex is talking about. I want to dislike every change and every new measure he puts into place, but this system is something I've been trying to get Mr. Waters to get since I started working here. This is going to be the only time I allow myself to think Alex is right about something though. And I am certainly not going to let him know I think he's right about this.

"Well, it seems like you two are getting along and I think I've done everything I need to do to hand over to you Alex," Mr. Waters says. "Unless either of you can think of anything else, I think I'll be getting off. If you think of anything later, you can always give me a call."

I can think of a hundred things that are all variations of don't leave me with this arrogant bastard, but I can't think of any genuine concern that I can voice to make him stay. Alex doesn't seem to have anything either and he shakes his head.

"Nothing from me," he says. "Catch you later Grandad."

I almost give Alex a piece of my mind for being so disrespectful and calling Mr. Waters grandad like that, but just in time, I remember that Mr. Waters is actually Alex's grandfather and Grandad is likely what he calls him as it's a bit less formal. I'm glad I remembered in time. As if Alex isn't going to be enough of a pain in my ass without me giving him ammunition to use against me.

I smile at Mr. Waters and hug him.

"Don't be a stranger," I say.

"I'm only ever a phone call away, Ros. Now promise me you'll keep this one in line," Mr. Waters replies.

"I promise," I say.

Keeping Alex in his place is something I think I might actually quite enjoy. His eye roll tells me he doesn't share the sentiment. Mr. Waters finally leaves, and Alex and I are alone. I kind of want to announce that I have work to do and go back to my desk, but professionalism stops me from just dropping Alex in the deep end and letting him flounder. I think the least I can do is offer him a tour of the building and get him up to speed with who is who here.

"Are you ready for a tour of the place?" I ask. "Or would you like to get settled in here first?"

"I think I can find my way around a four-floor building without a tour," Alex says.

"Of course you can," I agree. "And I'm sure you will also know who is who, and what each of them does, and who you need to keep an eye on as well as who will just get on with things. Need I go on?"

"You've made your point, but I'm sure you will still keep going on until your battery runs out," Alex says. "Ok, let's get this tour over with."

"I think it's great how you are really making an effort to get to know me and use my knowledge," I say.

"Just go," Alex says.

I turn toward the office door, and I roll my eyes. Today is going to be a long day and it's only going to be the first long day in a future filled with them. I open the door to Alex's office, and I jump when I see a man standing there, his back to the door. He's dressed in a black suit, and he turns around when he hears the door opening. He looks to be in his late thirties or early forties and his hair is short and dark brown. He has a square jaw, and his face is set in an expression of such perfect neutrality that he doesn't look real. He's kind of good-looking in a rough around the edges kind of way.

"Who are you? Why are you just standing here?" I ask.

"Ros, this is Will Maynard," Alex says from behind me. "He's my personal security guard and it's his job to stand at my door when I'm in my office. He will also be working on making the building as a whole more secure."

This is beyond unusual and for a moment, I'm speechless, just staring at Will and then I catch myself and give my head a small shake.

"Sorry," I say, holding my hand out. "I was just surprised, that's all."

"No problem," Will says, taking my hand and shaking it.

"Will shadows me so you'll get used to seeing him around

me, but honestly, just try to think of him as a part of the furniture," Alex says.

"Right," I say. "Because that's not rude at all."

"I prefer it that way," Will says. "It's hard to concentrate on my job if I'm constantly engaged in conversation."

"Ok, well if that's what you want, who am I to argue," I say.

I move past Will with Alex by my side, and we start walking along the hallway, Will behind us. The first thing I show Alex is the staff break room and the bathrooms for our personal use, and then I take him toward the other half of our floor.

"Does having a bodyguard make you feel important?" I say as we walk.

I know I shouldn't have said it, but I'm genuinely curious about why the hell Alex has a bodyguard and I don't want him to think I'm taking an interest. I much prefer him to think I'm just being snippy with him.

"No. It makes me feel safe," he replies.

I snort out a surprised laugh.

"Right. Because I'm sure there are millions of assassins lining up to take you out," I say.

"Maybe not millions, but some," Alex says. "My grandfather insisted on me having security after I was almost abducted and held for ransom."

I don't have an answer to that, and I'm glad that we have reached the first of the offices. I've been saved by the job, and I am grateful for that much. I take Alex along the line of offices, telling him who everyone is, what they do, and if there's anything specific that I think he needs to know about each person. He goes into each office to personally greet the person.

We move down through the rest of the floors, and as much as I hate to admit it, Alex is fair. He greets the low-level staff with the same smile and the same greeting as he did the higher management level staff. I guess it's just me he's going to be a dick to then. Oh well. He's met his match.

My cell phone rings, and I debate ignoring it. It hardly looks professional to have a friend call me in the middle of the working day on my new boss's first day here. But I know the secretaries from upstairs sometimes call me on my cell phone if I'm not at my desk. I decide to take the call and if it's a friend or family member, I will just talk to them as though they are a client. Alex won't know any different.

"Hello, Ros Thomas," I say, taking the call.

"Ros it's Selena. There's someone here to see Mr. Waters. The new Mr. Waters. She says she has an appointment," Selena says.

I was right to take the call then.

"What's her name?" I ask.

"Celia Morgan," Selena tells me.

"Hold on a second," I say.

I move my cell phone away from my face and turn my attention back to Alex.

"Have you set up any meetings I don't know about?" I ask.

"No, why?" he says.

"I have reception on the phone. There's a Celia Morgan to see you. Claims she has an appointment," I say.

"Oh Celia. Yes. Sorry I thought you meant client meetings. She's early," he says. He glances at his watch. "Oh. No, she isn't. We're late. Tell reception to have her wait in my office."

He starts walking away as I relay the message to Selena and end the call. He looks back over his shoulder.

"Well come on then," he says. "Stop messing around."

"I hardly think sorting out your visitor that you haven't put on the schedule or told anyone about counts as messing around," I say.

Alex shrugs one shoulder.

"Well, I would," he says.

Ugh. He's such a dick. I hate him. Even if I do keep getting a whiff of his expensive aftershave and wondering what it would smell like on my bed sheets.

"You can be a real asshole you know," I say as we get into the elevator to go back up to the fourth floor.

"So I'm told," Alex says. "And I always find my assholery reaches new levels when I'm around someone who thinks they're better than everyone else."

"Wait. You think I think that? I think you need to look in the mirror," I snap.

"I don't need to. I know I'm good-looking. And if I was unsure, the way you can't keep your eyes off me would remind me," Alex throws back.

"Don't flatter yourself," I say, although I am worried that the reddening of my cheeks will give away the truth that he is right. I had no idea he had noticed. But then a thought comes to me. "Anyway, if I was to be watching you, which I wasn't, and you know about it, surely that means you were looking back."

Ha. That will show him.

"I don't mind admiring a nice view," Alex says with a shrug. "It's only when you start talking that we have a problem."

He winks at me and steps off the elevator as the doors open. He leaves me a few paces behind him, my mouth hanging open in shock at his admission to watching me and his blatant rudeness. He must be used to the sort of women with no self-respect who want a man more the meaner he is to them. Well, that shit won't work on me.

"Are you ok Ros?" Will asks and I realize I'm still standing in the elevator car and Will is holding the door to stop it from closing.

"Yes. Sorry," I say, stepping out and thanking him for holding the door.

He gives me a nod of appreciation and I decide he's not so bad. Sure, he seems likely to be the strong silent type, but I guess that goes with the job, but when he asked me if I was ok, there was no trace of amusement on his face. If anything, he looked like he really was concerned.

I catch back up with Alex as we head for his office. I don't know why because truth be told, I would much rather walk beside Will. I guess I just don't want him to think he had gotten one up on me with his last shot.

I catch Alex looking at me out of the corner of his eye and he grins when he sees me catching him. I make a humph sound and I feel my cheeks redden again, but I don't make any comments, because I'm sure that Alex has a nice come back lined up and he's just waiting for me to walk into it so he can embarrass me further. Well, I won't give him that satisfaction.

"I caught you catching me looking," Alex says. "That must mean you were looking too. Admiring the view, were you?"

"More like just checking your head hadn't gotten too big to get through your office door," I say.

"Funny," Alex says.

"And yet you don't laugh. Oh, are you one of those men that think any sign of any emotion, including happy ones, is a weakness?" I ask. Before he can reply, I put on a fake, electronic toned voice. "I am a robot, and I will not laugh or smile."

Alex looks at me and although he still isn't smiling as such, I can see the amusement in his eyes as he watches me.

"Are you done?" he says.

"Yup," I reply.

"Good because I was almost ready to go looking for your off button," Alex says.

I swear that for a moment, the amusement in his eyes turns to lust, but no, that's got to just be wishful thinking on my part. Alex dislikes me. He's made that pretty clear. And anyway, I don't really think it is wishful thinking for me. I don't want Alex to find me attractive. Do I?

No, I really don't. It's bad enough that I'm so attracted to him physically without me starting to think he might feel the same way and flirting with him. He's probably trying to get me to do that so he can embarrass me some more. Well, he's not getting that satisfaction. Fuck him. God I'd love to fuck him. But I won't. Because if he wants it, I'd rather do without myself than give him anything he wants to have.

It's really annoying that his sarcastic words don't have as much effect on me as the way his mouth turns up slightly when he delivers them, or the way his eyes twinkle when he does laugh. And I'm sure I'm not the only one who can feel the tension in the air between us, and it isn't just the tension of two people who don't really like each other. It's more the tension of two people who want to fuck each other's brains out but are trying to hide the feeling. I wonder if Will has picked up on it. God, I hope not. I've just met the man. I don't want him thinking I'm some sort of sap that a man can be an absolute dick to and still have me salivating over him. Because I am not that person. Or at least I never was. No, I know my worth and I am not going to be someone's doormat.

We have reached Alex's office, and I no longer have to worry about Will's thoughts on the subject of Alex and me, because he waits outside of the office door again. Inside of the office is the woman that Selena called me about.

She looks to be about my age, twenty-eight, or maybe she's a little bit older than me. She has a short, blunt bob dyed bright red, and she's wearing a super tight black dress that is just long enough to be appropriate for the office rather than a nightclub. Her nails are long, and the shade of her nail varnish matches her hair and her high heels. Despite all of this though, she doesn't look cheap or tacky. In fact, she looks super sophisticated, and I wish I was half as put together as her on my best day, let alone at work.

The way her and Alex smile at each other tells me that they know each other on at least a friendly level, and I hope that's all it is. I really can't help but hope that this woman isn't his wife. I don't remember Mr. Waters mentioning Alex having a wife, but that doesn't necessarily mean he doesn't have one. I don't know why I care one way or the other, but the truth is, I do care. If he is married, I want her to be at least someone in my league, not this goddess.

"Ros, this is Celia Morgan. Celia, Ros Thomas," Alex says.

"Charmed I'm sure," Celia says as we shake hands. The way she looks me up and down tells me she is anything but charmed and I know on the fashion scale, I have just failed the test. Oh well. I'm a personal assistant not a model and Celia looks like the sort of woman who hates other women, so even if I was dressed head to toe in Armani, she would have turned her nose up at me.

"Celia came with me from my old company," Alex explains. "She was my assistant and I wanted her to come with me and be my assistant here but obviously my grandfather's clause prevented that, but we managed to get her a place on the management's reception team."

Celia looks me up and down again and this time, she actively smirks.

"So, you're the one who got my job," she says.

"No. I'm the one who has had this job for three years and you are the one who didn't make the grade to replace me," I reply.

I'm not having some jumped-up assistant coming in here

and calling the shots with me. It's one thing Alex doing it. As much as I hate it from him too, it is his job to call the shots with me; I am his assistant after all. It's most definitely not Celia's job to call the shots with me or anyone else for that matter.

Celia looks at me, an expression on her face that I imagine wouldn't look out of place if she had just stepped on a particularly large and crunchy cockroach. I hold her gaze, and inside I cheer when she is the one to look away first.

"I guess I'd best go and get started," she says to Alex, ignoring me completely now. "I just wanted to let you know that I'm here."

"Would you like me to come along and introduce you to the team?" I ask.

I know it makes it look like I'm trying to make an effort to be nice to Celia, but the truth is, I know that's the last thing she will want and now she will have to say no in a nice way, or she will look like a total asshole.

"Thanks, but I find introductions are a bit less awkward when they are less formal," she says with a forced smile.

"No worries. Just let me know if you need anything while you're getting settled in," I say.

"Thanks," she says again, her foxy looking smile staying in place, although the anger is clear to see in her eyes.

"Aww, she seems nice," I say once she's gone, leaving Alex in the same position, where he knows for a fact I'm being sarcastic, but on the surface, he can't prove I'm not just being nice. He makes a non-committal grunt that tells me everything I need to know about his understanding of my sarcasm.

It's more than obvious that Celia doesn't like me any more than Alex does, but to be honest, I don't care. She's jealous that I have the job she thought she was getting, which I can understand – Alex should never have promised her the job without talking to Mr. Waters first – but I think she also might have picked up on the tension between Alex and me and decided to make it clear she is against me too, just to lick Alex's ass.

"Unless you need anything, I'm going to go and get on with ordering that program for the messages," I say. "And if there's nothing before then, we have a meeting at two o'clock in the smaller conference room with representatives of Russel Howe Legal. We already do their accounting, but they are debating coming to us for payroll services too. Do you want me to lead the meeting, or have you got time to research Russel Howe and their needs and how we can help them?"

"I'll take care of it," Alex says. "I need an assistant, not a hand holder."

"As you wish," I say as I leave the office.

I'm torn as I sit down to start working. On the one hand, Alex is the most arrogant person I have met in a long time, and I want him to fall on his face so badly. But on the other hand, I really don't want to see everything Mr. Waters worked for go down the drain, and I think that's a big part of the reason Mr. Waters insisted I be kept on as Alex's assistant, because he knows that despite Alex's attitude, he actually is going to need a fair bit of hand holding, at least in the beginning, if he is to make this work.

CHAPTER
Two

ALEX

Just over a week has gone by since I took over the running of the company from my grandfather and I think I've been settling in quite well, even if I do say so myself. I know who most of the staff are and what they all do and where abouts in the building they work. I know the list of clients that my grandfather handled personally and what we do for each of them and why he handled them himself. I've met with the majority of them and introduced myself to them and reassured them that the service they receive will continue to be as good as ever or maybe even better. I've let them know I am always available if they need anything and just to call if they have any concerns. No one has called so I think that's a good thing.

The only thing I still haven't been able to do is get my head around is why my grandfather was so insistent that I keep Ros on as my assistant. I mean I'm not a monster. It's not like I wanted to fire her and throw her out onto the streets with nothing. I just wanted her to have the receptionist job and me to have an assistant I know and trust.

It shouldn't be long before I can get her out and Celia in as my assistant though. In fact, the first stage of that is on my desk in front of me; a report I requested from Ros that should have been a simple enough task but that has several mistakes in it. I personally find attention to detail to be an important skill, especially in my assistant, and if this turns out to be something Ros struggles with, then I feel like that's a valid reason that my grandfather can't argue with, even if he chose to put up with it.

I use the intercom on my desk phone to get Ros's attention. She answers my call.

"Hello?" she says.

"Can you come in here for a minute please," I say.

"Sure," Ros replies.

A couple of seconds later, my office door opens, and Ros appears in the doorway.

"Come on in and close the door," I say. I wait until she has done as I said and then I nod to the chair opposite mine on the other side of my desk. "Have a seat."

Ros sits down.

"Is everything ok?" she asks.

"Not really," I say with a sigh.

I push the papers on my desk closer to Ros and point to the first mistake in the report.

"What does that say?" I ask.

"Ninety-five," Ros replies. "But it should be eighty-five."

I go through the rest of the mistakes and for each one, she tells me exactly what it should be. I link my fingers together and rest my hands on my desk.

"Well, that proves you know your stuff," I say. I must admit I am actually surprised she knows all of these figures without having to look them up. I am not impressed though. I refuse to be impressed by her. "So, I can only assume the mistakes in the report are typos. Honestly Ros, I don't know if that's better or worse. It's better because you know the answers but it's worse that you have such a lack of attention to detail."

"Sorry, you lost me," Ros says.

I flick through the papers and show her the title page.

"This is your report, isn't it?" I ask.

"Yes," Ros replies. "But those mistakes weren't in it."

I raise an eyebrow.

"Are you saying I changed some of the numbers before I printed this out?" I ask.

"No, of course not," Ros says.

"So, you're saying someone in reception or in the IT department changed them then?" I ask. They are the only other departments that had access to the reports.

"No, but…" Ros says.

I interrupt her before she can go on.

"So, what happened then? Did the fairies come in and fuck this up?" I demand.

"I… I must have made those mistakes. I apologize Alex. I am always accurate with my figures. I don't know what happened," she says.

"I expect better Ros," I say. "My grandfather swore you are the best, better than Celia who I wanted to be my assistant, and yet Celia would never have made those kinds of mistakes."

"It's a good job that my role has a lot more to it than sending over reports then isn't it," Ros says.

For a moment when she was looking at the mistakes in the report and trying to work out how the hell she messed up something so simple, she actually looked sorrowful enough that I even started to feel a little bit sorry for her, but as she delivers her line about there being more to her role than reports, that cocky demeanor comes rushing back in. Her head tilts slightly and her top lip curls into a sneer. It's the look of someone with a major attitude problem and that is

Ros - she most definitely has a major attitude problem, although it seems to only be with me and Celia, but that's enough to get my back up.

She flicks her long, dark brown hair back and holds my gaze with brown eyes so dark they match her hair color perfectly. I know she's challenging me, waiting to see if I have any other grievances about her. I do, but none that are a sackable offense or even work related.

My other problem with Ros is as annoying as she is, there's something about her that I am drawn to. I look at the haughty angle of her head, the way her skirt and blouse caress her waif-like figure and hint at what's beneath them. My problem with Ros is that every time I look at her, all I want to do is swipe my desk clear, throw her on it, and fuck the attitude out of her.

"Is that everything?" Ros says after a moment of neither of us breaking eye contact.

I blink and then I curse myself inwardly for being the first one to look away.

"Yes," I say. "Fix this and get it back to me by the end of the day."

"I'll have it back to you within the next ten minutes unless anything urgent comes up," Ros says.

"And since when do you get to decide what is more important than the task that I have assigned you?" I ask.

"Since, hypothetically, a client needs something," she says.

She has me there and she knows it.

"Just go Ros before my patience with you runs out," I say.

It's not the best save, but it's better than nothing, I guess. Ros gets up and heads to my office door. I can't help but watch her ass sway beneath her skirt and I imagine myself rising up and getting to the door as she opens it, slamming it shut and fucking her up against it, her skirt around her hips, my hands all over her body.

I have to stop this, or Ros won't be the one making mistakes. I can't allow myself to become distracted by her, no matter how much I want her and no matter how much my cock comes to life at the sight of her. I wonder if I put 'give Alex a blow job' on her to do list for the day, she would do so. I think I know the answer to that one. Even if she didn't hate me, I don't think she would be up for sucking me off – it would mean she would have to shut up for a few minutes and I don't think she could handle that.

CHAPTER
Three

ROS

I sit at my desk, anger surging through me. I don't really know who I'm angrier with, whether it's Alex for pointing out my mistakes or whether it's me for making them in the first place. It has to be me, I think. Although I have no recollection of making those mistakes, I obviously did, and they were such fucking basic errors. But I suppose I wouldn't have a recollection of it, because if I did, then it means I knew they were mistakes, and I obviously would have fixed them before sending the reports to Alex. But they were such obvious mistakes, I just don't see how I could have made them. It's not like they were mistakes in the math which I guess could be forgivable. It was a mistake typing the right figures down, something I'm pretty sure you could teach a monkey to do. And apparently, I struggle with it.

What if I have always been this careless, and Mr. Waters just used to fix my errors without telling me. No, that's ridiculous. Maybe down the line, when we had worked together a long time and I had proved myself to him, he would have done that if I made one typo, but he wouldn't have put up with it if it was constant and it was that many mistakes. He is a nice guy but he's no pushover.

This leads me back to thinking that maybe I wasn't the one to fuck up. I can't help but wonder if someone else made the mistake. It was Alex who made me consider the idea actually. I know he was being sarcastic when he asked me if I thought one of the receptionists or one of the IT guys had tampered with the report, but what if they had? What if Celia got her perfectly manicured little hands on it and decided to try and sabotage me? I don't think I would put it past her. She's made it clear she doesn't like me and that she thinks my job should rightfully be hers. Would she go to these lengths to get me out of the way and get my job?

I don't know for sure, but I'm going to keep a very close eye on her from now on. I am not going to talk to Alex about this yet though. I would be crazy to tell him I even suspect such a thing, because he is hardly my biggest fan, and to talk badly about his golden girl Celia, won't go down too well I don't think. No, I'll wait until I have some sort of proof of what Celia is doing before I go to Alex about it, and then if I have proof, he won't be able to do anything except act on it and I will look vindicated instead of paranoid.

That's assuming that firstly she did do it. And that secondly, she does it again. I don't know whether she will or not. I think she will still be coming for me, but I think she will try a different tactic this time. I don't think she'll keep on doing the same thing over and over again. I think she might try it once more and then she'll move on to something else. As long as it's nothing that affects any clients, I can let it play out until I catch her red handed. I don't mind playing the long game, as long as I'm in it to win. Celia has chosen the wrong person to fuck around with.

~

I take my cell phone out of my purse and drop my keys into it. I hang my purse and my jacket on the hooks by the door and kick my shoes off beneath them. It feels good to be home and even better to be out of those heels. I take a moment to let my feet appreciate the fact they are no longer being contorted and then I head out of the tiny entrance hall and into the main living area of my apartment.

The living area is an open plan living room, dining room and kitchen with a sliding glass door leading outside to a small balcony. Another door leads to a hallway where there are two large bedrooms, a big bathroom and a smaller second bathroom, and a couple of cupboards. I know I'm lucky to have such a good-sized apartment in a nice neighborhood and I also know I wouldn't be able to afford a place like this on my own without spending a lot more of my trust fund than I want to at this point in my life, which makes me even more grateful for my roommate and best friend, Fiona McLopin.

I know some people who are best friends but who would fall out with each other if they had to live together but living together only made Fiona and me closer. Fiona was one of the first people I met when I came to New York at eighteen to go to college here and although I always planned on going back home, by the time college ended, I felt like this city was my home and I stayed on here.

"Glass of wine?" I say to Fiona now as a way of greeting her as I head toward the kitchen.

Fiona turns around on the couch to face me. She nods her head.

"Why not," she says. "I guess you had a bad day?"

"You could say that," I say as I reach up to the glassware cabinet and get two wine glasses out. I go to the fridge and pull out a bottle of white wine. A quick glance at the label tells me it is Sauvignon Blanc. Whatever. I don't profess to be some sort of wine connoisseur. If it tastes nice, I drink it. If it doesn't, I'd like to say I don't, but truthfully, I would probably drink it anyway. It would be a shame to let it go to waste.

I pour out two large measures and put the rest back in the fridge. I already know it won't still be there by the end of the night, but it might as well be cold when we inevitably go for our refills. I take the two glasses to the living room and hand one to Fiona who has turned back to face the TV, although she has muted the volume. I sit down in the armchair that I always take, and we both have a drink of the wine and then put our glasses down on the coffee table.

"What happened?" Fiona asks.

"Alex happened. Or Celia happened. Some fucker happened," I say angrily.

Fiona waits for me to explain further. That's something I love about Fiona. She gives me time to process my thoughts and choose the right words instead of hurrying me along when I'm venting to her about things.

"I wrote a report Alex asked me for and today, he pulled me into his office and showed me several mistakes in it," I say. "I know I'm not perfect and of course I could make a mistake, but not that many in one report, and not ones that I spotted easily and knew the correct information for without having to look it up."

I lean forward and take another drink of my wine. I feel slightly better as it cools my throat on the way down. I sit back again, my legs tucked beneath me.

"I'm convinced I didn't make those mistakes," I say. "The only people with access to that document was me, Alex and the reception team. Oh, and the IT department technically has access to everything on the system, but they have no reason to open reports or be poking around in them, and they have always been able to access files, but they've never pulled a stunt like this before. On the other hand, Celia is a part of that reception team and it's no secret she wants my job."

"You think she changed things in your report to make you look bad?" Fiona asks.

I shrug my shoulders.

"No. Yes. I don't know. Yes," I say. I might as well be honest with Fiona. Doing so won't get me fired and if the idea is ridiculous, she will be the first one to say so. "Yes. I think she did. Because those mistakes weren't in that report when I sent it and no one else at the company has a reason to try and make me look bad. Plus, the other receptionists have been with the company for ages. Why would they do this now when we all get along?"

Fiona is quiet for a moment. She picks her wine up and sips it thoughtfully. I wait patiently for her to digest the information I've just laid on her for all of about three seconds and then I can't stand the silence any longer.

"If you think I'm being crazy or paranoid, just say so," I say.

"I don't think that at all," Fiona says. "I was trying to come up with some way you could get concrete proof of what she's done, because without it, you can't really accuse her to your boss, especially with them being old friends."

Relief floods me, making me feel all warm inside. Or maybe that's the wine. Either way, I feel better for knowing that Fiona doesn't think I'm paranoid or I'm just in denial about making those mistakes.

"Definitely not," I say. "The bastard even had the nerve to say that Celia wouldn't have made those kinds of mistakes if she had done the report."

"Are they fucking each other?" Fiona asks casually.

I consider it and then I shake my head.

"I don't get that impression, no. I genuinely believe that Alex wanted to bring in his own assistant and I am the one person standing in the way of that, hence the fact he hates me. I think Celia must know this too and she must also know that if she can create a scenario where any reasonable person would fire me, she gets my job," I say.

"So basically, what you're saying is that if you bring up this theory without proof, Alex will take Celia's side," Fiona says. "And he might even use that as grounds to fire you, like saying not only are you making silly mistakes but then you're trying to pass the blame for them off onto other people. So, we need to go carefully, and we need to catch the bitch out. And we have an advantage. She doesn't know that we know that she's trying to sabotage you."

"That's true," I say. "Meaning that she's more likely to get careless. She'll get cocky and that's when I'll be able to catch her out. But how long will that take? I told myself earlier I was happy to play the long game, but you know me, Fi. I don't know if I can keep quiet and pretend like I don't know what's happening for very long. And also, what if I get fired in the meantime?"

"We need like a reverse blind copy," Fiona says.

"Huh?" I grunt, unsure what she means.

"You know, like if you were to send her an email and only put her email address in the recipient bar but then blind copy the boss in so he can see her being a bitch. Like that only backward. We need to send an email that only Celia will have access to but have her think everyone else in reception can see it. At the same time, send a copy of the email to Alex so he can see the original report or whatever it is before Celia has a chance to change anything. And then when she sabotages you, there's your proof it's her," Fiona says.

I think for a moment as I drink the last bit of my wine and put my empty glass down on the coffee table.

"There might be a way I can do that," I say. "Well not that exactly, but something that will have the same effect. I'll need to find an excuse to email Celia about something which I can do easily enough. And then when I send the report, I'll send it only to her instead of to the whole reception team. She will hopefully not notice and just assume the whole team has it. Then the rest of the plan goes down as you said. And me having emailed her a few days ago is my cover story in case she does notice and questions it. I can just say she was at the top of my used contacts, and I didn't realize and accidentally sent it to just her instead of the team."

"Perfect," Fiona says with a wicked little grin. "Make sure you keep copies of your sent emails in case Alex tries to cover Celia's back and you have to get HR involved. They will be impartial hopefully, but they won't act without proof so make sure you have it."

"I will," I say, returning her grin.

Fiona stands up and picks up my glass along with her own almost empty glass.

"We need to toast to this plan. It's far too good for us not to," she says.

She downs the last bit of her wine and then she goes to the fridge and refills our glasses, leaving out the now empty wine bottle. She comes back and hands me my glass back then she sits down with her own, which she holds in the air.

"To Ros taking back her power and showing this little Celia bitch how things work around here," Fiona says.

"Cheers to that," I say, tapping my glass lightly against hers.

We drink and then we both start to laugh, and I realize how much better I feel. Partly I'm sure because I now have a plan to put into place, but also, I think, because Fiona has managed to make me laugh at a time when I was sure laughter was the furthest thing from my mind.

CHAPTER Four

ROS

My desk phone rings, and I glance down to see the blue light that indicates it's an intercom call, in other words, it's Alex calling me from his office. I pick the receiver up and bring it up to my ear.

"Hi Alex," I say.

"Can you send me the file for Blackwood's please?" Alex says.

"Sure," I reply.

I'm curious as to why he wants it. Blackwood's is one of those clients who never rocks the boat, and his account just trundles along nicely. No one from the company has called or visited and it seems weird that Alex would want to see the file, but I know if I question it, he not only won't tell me what he wants with the file, he will make sure I know I'm crossing a line even asking about it. In one sense, I would just be being nosy, but in another sense, if there is a reason he wants the file, I actually might be able to help him, but fuck it. He always thinks the worst of me so let him do his own information dive if he needs it.

I go into the archives on my computer and find the file

and send it across to Alex. He pings over a thank you and I go back to what I was doing before he called through. An uneventful hour passes and then my phone rings again, and again the intercom light is on. I answer the call, but before I can speak, Alex speaks.

"My office. Now," he says, and the line goes dead.

I debate not going, just telling him I didn't hear him and when I tried to ask him to say it again, he had ended the call, but he sounded really pissed off and to be honest, I don't want to make it any worse for myself by adding to his anger. I have no idea what he wants me for, or what has gone wrong to have him sound so annoyed.

I get up and head for the office, smiling a greeting at Will who stands at his usual post. He nods his head to me, and I go into the office. Alex is behind his desk looking as hot as ever, despite the anger in his eyes.

"What is it?" I ask as I make my way toward him.

"Why does it seem like you can't do even the simplest of tasks correctly?" he says.

"Excuse me," I say, taken aback by the venom in his words and the untruth of them too.

I sit down without waiting to be asked and I wait for Alex to explain what the hell he is talking about.

"I have spent the last hour updating this file because I have a meeting scheduled with the client for next week and I wanted to have the most up to date information in there. I decided to do the update myself after your mess up on the last report I asked you for, because I wanted to be certain it was right. I didn't think there was any way you could screw this up if I was the one doing the updates. But you managed it didn't you?" Alex says.

His voice climbs in volume on the last couple of words and I involuntarily shrink back a little bit. I force myself to sit up straight and look him in the eye. I won't let him think I'm afraid of him, or even remotely affected by his temper.

"I'm sorry, I don't know what you're getting at. How can I have made a mistake in the file if you updated it?" I say, genuinely confused.

"You sent me the wrong fucking file," Alex yells. "I asked for the Lockwood file, and you sent me the Blackwood file."

"That's not true," I say quickly. "I specifically remember you asking for the Blackwood file, because I thought it was odd because Blackwood's is one of those clients we never really hear from and never have a problem with."

"So, you misheard me. That's all you have to say Ros. You don't have to get all defensive like this," Alex says. He no longer sounds angry. He sounds condescending and it gets my back up more than him shouting at me, but I force myself to stay calm. I will not yell and curse and give him an excuse to give me a warning for insubordination.

"I heard you just fine. You asked for the Blackwood file," I say, keeping my voice and tone calm and quiet.

"Look Ros, I know what I asked for. Why would I want to see the Blackwood file when I don't have anything upcoming with them and a simple check on the system would show that and also would show that I do have a meeting with a representative from Lockwood's. Common sense says you should have questioned it," Alex says.

"I almost did," I say. "But I was afraid you would tell me to mind my own business."

"I'm not going to tell you to mind your own business for asking for clarification on a task Ros and the very idea that I might is ridiculous. Look I'm not saying you did this on purpose, but I need you to be more careful in the future. This has been a waste of my time, and now it will be a further waste of my time putting it all right. And then you further waste my time by making silly excuses and arguing with me," Alex says.

"I'll put the file right," I say, ignoring all the things I actually want to say and settling on the one that won't get me fired instead.

Alex shakes his head.

"No. I need to know this is done correctly so I will do it. And I will get the Lockwood file myself when I'm done with this. Seriously Ros, you need to get your head in the game, because if it gets to the point where I'm regularly doing your job because I don't trust you to get it right, then what exactly will I need you for?" Alex says.

"I'm sorry," I say. "I'll do better."

It's the best I can manage to get out through my gritted teeth and Alex seems to accept it, because he nods his head and points to the door. I get up and leave the office without either of us saying another word. I go back to my desk, so angry I feel like I need to scream or punch something. Or someone. Maybe Celia is right in her smug, perfectly made-up little face. Except this time, I can't blame Celia. Either Alex said the wrong name, or I did indeed mishear him. I personally think it's the former, but either way, if this was the only mistake that got made, I wouldn't be thinking anything of it, but with Celia's sabotages as well, it all adds up and I know I need to be extra careful about everything and also find a way to get my plan to out Celia moving ahead and quickly.

CHAPTER
Five

ALEX

Will and I step out of the elevator and head along the corridor toward my office. I can see Ros sitting at her desk already and I have to fight to take my eyes off of her. She has her hair up today and her neck looks so kissable, and I can't help but picture her naked, me behind her, kissing her neck as I fuck her.

As we approach her desk, she looks up. She smiles at Will who returns her smile and then she looks at me and her smile fades away. Charming. Although I do share her sentiment. If she wasn't so easy on the eye, I wouldn't exactly relish seeing her sitting here either.

"Alex, you have an emergency meeting at ten o'clock with Lance Donovan," Ros says.

I go over to her desk and Will turns away, standing guard and trying to look as though he can't hear every word we're saying. Not that it matters. I trust Will completely.

"What? Why on earth would you authorize that without checking with me first?" I ask.

"Because you weren't here yet and if I didn't agree to a meeting with you this morning, he was going to take his business elsewhere. It was all I could do to make it ten o'clock and not earlier so at least we have time to go over his account and get you up to speed on it all," Ros says.

"And why is this man so important he gets to call the shots like this?" I demand.

"Because he is the CEO of Brannigan's, and they are our biggest client. Their work accounts for over twenty five percent of our takings," Ros says calmly.

Oh fuck. This doesn't sound good. It also means I have to eat humble pie after snapping at Ros for scheduling the meeting.

"Ok. You did the right thing," I say. "Did you manage to get anything out of him about what he wants?"

Ros looks taken aback at my confirmation that she did the right thing. Am I really that horrible to her all the time that she's surprised when I acknowledge something that she did right? Maybe I am. Maybe I should feel bad about it – after all it's not her fault my grandfather insisted that she be kept on in this role - but now isn't the time for shit like that. I have to sort out whatever this mess is first. And anyway, if I get my way, it's not like Ros is going to be here for much longer so I guess it doesn't really matter whether she thinks I appreciate her efforts or not. That won't be her fault either, but business is business and sometimes we have to do things we don't particularly like doing in order to get the right results.

"No. I did try to, but he didn't want to discuss it over the phone, and he was so angry I didn't want to make him angrier by pushing him for an answer," Ros tells me. "He had a really good working relationship with Mr. Waters, and I don't think he's too happy that he's left the company, but there's more to it than that. He did say he would give you a chance so he wouldn't threaten to leave unless there was something serious going on."

SURVIVING THE NEW BOSS 49

"Ok," I say. "Well, I'll try and get to the bottom of it before he gets here. I trust his file has already been sent over?"

Ros nods her head.

"Yes. Should I give you five minutes to look over it and then come in?" she says.

"Why do you want to come in? Isn't it something that can wait until after the meeting?" I ask.

"It's about the meeting," Ros says. "I was just going to give you a head's up about Lance Donovan, so you know what sort of things to discuss with him. On a personal level I mean."

I shake my head.

"That won't be necessary, thank you," I say. "I know my grandfather liked all that touchy feely stuff with the clients, but I don't work like that. I like a professional relationship only and I think most clients are happy with that."

"I..." Ros starts.

I hold my hand up and she has the good sense to stop talking.

"I'll be doing this my way," I say.

"If that's what you want," Ros says, and I nod. "I trust you will still want refreshments?"

"Yes," I say. "I want to be professional, not rude."

I go to my office before she can start bleating on about the way my grandfather did things and how I should do it his way and all that malarkey. Don't get me wrong, I respect my grandfather greatly and I don't deny that his methods worked. But they worked for him because that is his personality. I'm not exactly the warm and fuzzy type and clients aren't stupid. They see through all of that if it's fake and what might be a personal touch when it's genuine, becomes something icky when it's fake.

I sit down at my desk and fire up my computer and load the file for Brannigan's. I quickly familiarize myself with their account with us and what we do for them. It all looks like pretty standard stuff although the account is massive with lots of sister companies all under the one umbrella. There is nothing that jumps out at me as something that would class as an emergency. No deadlines have been missed or anything like that, and there hasn't been any unexpected contact from the IRS or anything like that.

I check the time. It's nine forty-five and I'm no closer to knowing what this is going to be about than I did when I walked into the building. I flip through the file one more time and it hits me like a fist to the gut.

There, right in the middle of the profit and loss column is a glaring mistake. A glaring mistake that makes it look as though we have cost Brannigan's an extra three million dollars in taxes. Of course we haven't done any such thing, but the CEO wouldn't know that if he had chosen to look at the figures on our shared drive today which he obviously did for whatever reason.

This file is one of the ones I switched out a figure or two on ready to be able to blame Ros for making the mistake and give me another black mark against her name that would soon add up to a reason to fire her so that Celia could become my assistant instead. I guess when I came to put the mistakes right again after not being able to wangle in a way to use them yet, I missed one. And of course, it had to be one that makes us look like total idiots to our biggest client, because why wouldn't the universe fuck with me that way.

Fuck. Fuck. Fuckity fuck.

I'm in deep shit here and I only have myself to blame for it. I can't even use this against Ros now. It would be perfect if I could, because if something nearly costs us our biggest client (or does cost us the client, although I'm not wanting to go there yet) that would definitely be a sackable offense that even my grandfather couldn't argue with. The trouble is, Ros hasn't accessed the file until this morning to send it to me, and when she obviously denies making the mistake, HR won't just fire her without looking into it and the logs from IT will show that the only person who has been in the Brannigan file except their usual accountant that could have messed up the figures is me.

I'm just going to have to tell Lance Donovan that a mistake was made and has now been rectified and apologize and hope to God he accepts that. I quickly change the figures back to what they should read as I think about this. Imagine how embarrassing it would be having him come in and me having to admit to him that there's been a mistake made and then having to tell him that I still haven't bothered to fix it, even now that I have noticed it.

At one minute to ten o'clock, there's a knock on my office door. I take a deep breath, straighten my tie, and call out 'come in'. My office door opens, and Ros stands there.

"Mr. Lance Donovan for you," she says.

"Thank you, Ros. Please send him in," I say.

Ros stands back and a man comes in. He looks to be in his mid to late fifties. He's wearing a gray suit and a white shirt. He's tall and well-built and his face is bright red as though he has been running, although I doubt he has done more than catch the elevator and walk along the corridor.

"Mr. Donovan," I say, standing up and extending my hand as he reaches my desk. "It's a pleasure to meet you. I'm Alex Waters."

Mr. Donovan shakes my offered hand and grunts a greeting. He sits down without being asked which annoys me, but I don't let it show.

"I do believe I have found the reason for the meeting," I start. "I was going through your figures before the meeting, and I spotted an anomaly which has now obviously been fixed. Please accept my most sincere apologies and my guarantee that this won't happen again."

"But here's the thing son," Mr. Donovan says. Son. Is he fucking kidding me right now? It takes every bit of self-control I have to not comment on him calling me that. "It shouldn't have happened in the first place and yet it did. Under your watch. Why would I trust you to make sure it doesn't happen again? Also, let's be honest here, you never would have found that mistake if I hadn't asked for this meeting, would you?"

"Honestly? No, I wouldn't have found the mistake today. But I have every confidence that it would have been spotted before your paperwork was filed," I say.

"Well, I'm glad you're confident about that son, because I'm not. Not anymore," he says. "When your grandfather told me he was handing the company over to his grandson, everything in me told me to get out then, that you would come in here with all these big ideas and let the little things, the things that matter to clients, slip. But I chose to give you the benefit of the doubt, and at least now I don't have to feel bad about pulling my business away."

As he is speaking, my office door opens, and Ros comes in with two steaming mugs. She puts mine down in front of me and Mr. Donovan's down in front of him.

"It seems this will be the last time you make me a coffee Ros love," Mr. Donovan says.

"Oh no, don't say that," Ros says. She perches on the chair beside Mr. Donovan. "What's happened? I'm sure we can fix it."

"Once the trust is gone, there's not much that can be done in the way of fixing things," Mr. Donovan replies.

"Fair point," Ros says. "Anyway, how's Barbara?"

"She's good. Better than good in fact," Mr. Donovan says. "She's on at me to retire soon, but she has the little rugrats over all the time, and don't get me wrong, I love my grandkids from the bottom of my heart, but it feels a lot more like hard work looking after them than coming to the office does."

Ros laughs along with Mr. Donovan. I glare at her and then make a point of looking at the door. I know she gets the message that I want her to leave, but she ignores it and I silently fume. It would look too unprofessional for me to actually ask her to leave in the middle of her talking to a client, but I really need to get this meeting back on track and find out what I can do to save this account.

"I can well imagine it," Ros says. "They must be what? Nine and seven now?"

"Yes," Mr. Donovan says. "And Sherry has another one on the way, so no doubt we'll have a baby staying over soon too."

"That might work in your favor. Barbara might want to hand them back after a few sleepless nights Lance," Ros laughs.

My eyes widen as he laughs with her, not correcting her about the casual use of his first name.

"Now if you ask me, you have enough going on to give you sleepless nights without messing around looking for another accountant. So why don't you tell us what we can do to make you trust us again," Ros says.

I am so mad I can just about feel steam coming out of my ears like on a cartoon. As if he's going to talk business with my assistant and even if he tells her a bit about it, if he won't accept an apology from me, the CEO, he's certainly not going to do so from Ros.

"There was a mistake on my profit and loss sheet. A mistake that would have cost me around three million dollars if it had gone to the IRS like that," Mr. Donovan says, surprising me by telling Ros that much.

"And I suppose Alex has been too modest to tell you he fixed it?" she says.

"No, he told me he fixed it. But putting a figure right isn't enough Ros. How can I be sure it won't happen again," Mr. Donovan says.

"That's because Alex only told you half the story Lance," Ros says. Again, I feel my anger flare up at the way she has come in here and taken over the meeting, but Mr. Donovan is eating out of Ros's hand, and I decide to sit back and see where this goes. At this point, I don't think we stand a chance of getting his business back because it's all been so unprofessional so I might as well watch how this pans out. "When Alex found the mistake, he got straight onto working out who made it, and it turned out to be an intern who – how shall I put this? – has had less than the desirable attitude since coming here. Alex fired him on the spot. I know why you're angry and I know why you feel like the trust is gone, but please be assured that nothing the interns do is ever filed without being checked first. The file was in the pile to be checked, and it just happened that you got to it before we did."

"Why the hell didn't you tell me you fired the person responsible so it can't happen again?" Mr. Donovan demands of me, and I have no answer, but Ros doesn't give me a chance to look like I don't have one.

"Isn't it obvious Lance? Mr. Waters has told Alex how he treated everyone here like family and how his clients loved that about him. He didn't want to tell you he had fired someone and make it look like we're no longer that close knit unit," Ros says.

"Well, I suppose I can understand that. But a family unit only works when all the members pull their weight and sometimes you have to cut a member or two," Mr. Donovan says.

I can tell he's softening, and I want to say something, but I'm scared anything I say will have the opposite effect than what I want, and I again sit back and let Ros do her thing.

"Please Lance, give us one more chance," Ros says.

Mr. Donovan goes quiet for a moment and then he speaks again.

"There are two conditions," he says. "One, you always make me coffee this good."

He flashes Ros a grin and I know then that everything is going to be ok with this client. He wouldn't be cracking jokes about his coffee if he was still truly pissed off. He just wants a chance to throw his weight around for a moment, so it looks like he didn't give in too easily. Ros nods her agreement to his coffee statement.

"And the second one is a little bit more serious," he goes on. "Ros, I want your word that you personally will double check my accounts with Alex here before anything is filed. At least until I get to know and trust him. Do we have a deal?"

"I'm happy with that as long as Alex is," Ros says.

"Of course," I say. I smile at Mr. Donovan. "Thank you for giving us a second chance Mr. Donovan."

"Lance," he says, smiling back at me.

"Lance," I repeat. "If there's anything you need, or anything I can do for you. Please do let me know."

"Thanks son," Lance says.

I still don't like him calling me son, but it's not quite so bad now that he's not berating me as he calls me it. We both stand up and shake hands and Ros stands up too.

"I'll walk you out," she says.

"Can you come back in here when you're done there, please Ros," I say.

She nods her head and the two of them leave my office and I breathe a loud sigh of relief. I'd like to say I saved the account, but truthfully, Ros saved it. I know in that moment I won't be sabotaging Ros anymore for two reasons. Firstly, it nearly came back to bite me in the ass in a big way there. And secondly, I was only doing it because I believed Celia would be a better assistant to me than Ros would be, and I see now that I was wrong about that. Celia is damned good, but she never would have pulled that off. It's time for me to admit that I do need Ros after all, and I think it might also be time for me to start being a bit nicer to her now that I'm not actively trying to push her out of her job.

Less than five minutes pass and Ros reappears in my office doorway. She is already talking as she comes in.

- "Look I'm sorry ok. I know I overstepped the mark, but I just didn't want us to lose the client, and-" Ros says.

"Ros stop," I interrupt her, and she does as I say.

She's still standing in the office doorway and that's ok. I only want to say one thing and then she can go.

"I didn't ask you to come back here so I could tell you off," I say. "I wanted to thank you. You saved that account, and I am more than grateful to you."

"Oh. Ok. Umm, you're welcome," Ros stutters.

She flushes slightly and then she leaves my office, leaving me fantasizing about how her cheeks will be flushed like that when I have finished fucking her. God, I need to get these thoughts out of my head one way or the other.

CHAPTER
Six

ROS

Things seem to have settled down around the office. It looks like Celia has gotten bored of trying to sabotage me. She must have seen it wasn't getting her the results she desired and gave up. I'm pleased about this obviously, but I can't help but be disappointed in Celia. She doesn't have the staying power I gave her credit for. She is still vile to me though so maybe she thinks she will eventually get rid of me that way, but what she doesn't know about me is I have to like a person, or at least have a modicum of respect for them, for their words to have any effect on me. So needless to say, Celia's poisonous words really don't worry me at all.

Since Alex's meeting with Lance Donovan and me saving him as a client, Alex has been a bit nicer to me. By which I mean he isn't constantly having a go at me. He's still not exactly friendly but that's ok – I don't think I'm ready to be friends with him just because he's decided it's time to stop being mean to me. I think he likely realized during that meeting that I do actually have my uses to the company, and it probably helps that Celia's sabotages have stopped too, because it means that I don't look like I'm making lots of stupid mistakes.

All in all, I'm finally being left alone to get on with my job and that's just how I like it. Obviously, Alex still gives me lists of tasks he wants completed, but now that's all he does. He doesn't try to tell me exactly how to do each one, or which order to do them in unless some are genuinely pressing, and he doesn't hover over me checking everything I do. He gives me the list and trusts that it will be done and that if there is anything I need to clarify with him, that I will do that. He has even started to listen to me a little bit in relation to clients and staff members, like if he is planning on doing something and I tell him that they won't respond to that way of working, but if he does it this other way they will, he actually is doing things the way I recommend.

I guess what I'm saying is that things have calmed down and the office is running as an office should again. Not everyone has to like each other, but everyone has to be civil to each other and get the job done. Now all I need to do to make every day even better is to get over this damned crush I have on Alex. I just can't shake it. It doesn't help that he's not actively being a massive dick to me anymore; that just means I can now imagine fucking him because I find him attractive rather than just thinking of myself hate fucking him.

Alex's office door opens, and I feel my cheeks flush at the sight of him at such a moment where I was thinking of fucking him. It's not like he knows what I was thinking obviously, but that doesn't stop me from feeling a little bit embarrassed.

"What's wrong?" Alex asks, approaching my desk. "You look all flustered."

"Nothing," I say quickly. "I'm just a bit warm. Are you warm? Is it warm in here today?"

I know I'm babbling, and I force myself to be quiet.

"Are you sure you're ok?" Alex says with a frown.

I'd be a whole lot better if he stopped talking and put his lips to better use on my body. I clear my throat and force myself to be professional.

"I'm sure. What can I do for you?" I ask, and I don't let that little voice inside of me, the one that seems to want to get me in trouble answer with anything dirty, although it tries to, and I just have to ignore it.

"I've just had a call from Lance Donovan. He wants another meeting," Alex says. "But this time, he wants it at his country club over dinner."

I can't help but roll my eyes. What is it with rich men and their little clubs?

"I know," Alex says with a flash of a grin. "I'm not a fan of those places either. But he's the client so he gets to choose the location of our meetings. Anyway, he wants you along. Tonight, at seven thirty."

For a moment I'm pissed off that Alex thinks he can just demand to have dinner with me and assume that I have no plans of my own for the evening. I mean I don't, but that's not the point. I tell myself it's not really him; he's just the messenger here. It's Lance who expects me to show up just because he said so and I know Lance well enough to know he won't have considered whether or not I have plans, and even if he did consider it, he would expect me to cancel them to look after his needs.

I want to say no. Even aside from the assumption I'll be available or willing to make myself so, I really don't want to spend an evening in the company of Lance and Alex. Lance is a nice enough man, and Alex I guess isn't the worst company in the world (although he's probably top ten), but they aren't people I would ever choose to socialize with. I know I don't really have a choice though. Unfortunately, it comes with the job. If a client wants me in a meeting, I'm expected to be in the meeting, even if it is on an evening.

"I'll be there," I say with a sigh. "What's the address of the place?"

"Don't worry about that. I'll send a car to pick you up at seven," Alex says.

"Ok, thanks," I say.

"And do me a favor Ros. By the time the dinner rolls around, make a better job at hiding the fact you clearly don't want to be there," he says.

"Oh really?" I say, my voice full of mock innocence. "But I thought the client would like to know I don't want to be there."

Will makes a snorting sound from his spot by Alex's office door, which he turns into a cough, but I'm almost certain it was a laugh. Alex glares at him for a second, and I think he suspects the same thing, but he can't prove it and so he can't say anything to Will.

"Just leave your usual self at home and try to be a little bit charming," Alex says.

"I will if you do," I say.

Alex rolls his eyes and goes back into his office, slamming the door behind him, and this time, there is no doubting the sound coming from Will is a laugh.

CHAPTER Seven

ROS

I spritz a final spray of perfume across my chest and then I think again and quickly go for a spray behind each ear as well. I check myself in the mirror. I'm wearing a black dress that sits an inch or two above my knee. The dress cuts in at the waist and it has a sweetheart neckline and thin straps. I've matched it with black stilettos with high, silver heels and a black and silver clutch bag. I've curled my hair and accessorized with a silver necklace, bracelet and earrings. It's hard to get the right balance of dressed up and professional when you are going somewhere people dress fancy but are going there for a business meeting, but I think I've just about gotten it right.

It's a few minutes to seven o'clock anyway, so I don't have time to change even if I wanted to. I pick my clutch bag up and slip my keys, some cash, my credit card and my cell phone into it, and then I leave my bedroom and go toward the living room to wait for my car.

I'm startled when I enter the living room and see Fiona in the kitchen cooking herself dinner.

"I didn't hear you come in," I say.

"Shit Ros, you scared me. I didn't even know you were home," Fiona says, and then she turns around and her jaw drops when she sees me. "Wow. Look at you. You look gorgeous. I guess I know the answer to my question about whether or not you want some dinner."

"I have a meeting with Alex and a client," I say. "The client wanted to do it over dinner."

"Ah, so a date then," Fiona teases me.

I know I shouldn't bite, but I do.

"I don't know how dates work in your world, but in mine, I don't invite clients along," I say.

"But at some point, he will leave, right?" Fiona says.

"Right. And so will I," I say.

Fiona smirks.

"I'm not buying it," she says. "No one wears those shoes unless they want to look sexy."

I start to argue the point, but before I can say much, the intercom buzzes.

"That will be my car," I say, heading for the door. "See you later."

"Have fun," Fiona says. "Don't do anything I wouldn't do."

"That doesn't cancel much out," I grin.

Fiona grins back.

"Well, I did say have fun," she says.

We're both laughing as I exit the apartment and go down to the lobby and out to my waiting car, where the driver stands beside the rear door, which he opens for me when I reach the car. I thank him and get in and he closes the door gently and gets into the driver's seat. He closes his door, starts up the engine, and pulls away and joins the flow of traffic and I sit back and relax, getting my head into the game and going into charming, workplace Ros mode.

It's not as hard as I feared it would be. Somehow dressing

up always makes me feel better and I have decided to make the best of the situation. Country clubs might not be my first choice of place, but generally speaking, they do a nice meal so at least there's that.

By the time my driver pulls up outside of the place, I've let go of my irritation at having to be here, and instead, I'm quite curious as to what Lance wants to discuss that would need to include me and be in depth enough that he wants a full evening meal through which to discuss it.

I thank the driver as he opens my door for me. I get out of the car and head toward the entrance to the country club as my driver closes the door and gets back in the car and drives away. I step inside the country club. The décor is old school luxury, all oak paneling and deep reds and golds. There is a small bar opposite the entrance with a few seats which I assume is an area to wait for a table to be ready, and then the dining area is to the left and to the right is a larger bar area for relaxing in.

To my immediate right is a small, dark wood colored lectern behind which stands a man in the same black trousers, white shirt and black waistcoat as the other staff I can see in the place. He smiles at me as I glance at him.

"Can I help you ma'am?" he says.

"I'm here for dinner," I say. "I think the reservation will be under Lance Donovan."

The man pulls a tablet from his pocket and checks it and then he nods his head.

"Follow me Ms. Thomas," he says, coming out from behind the lectern.

I follow him into the dining room and spot Alex and Lance already seated at a window table. Lance stands up and waves and I wave back. When I reach the table, Alex stands up too and I can't help but notice him checking me out. Ok, so maybe I did want to be a little bit sexy tonight, and I am glad Alex noticed.

My escort pulls out a chair for me and I sit down, and he tucks me underneath the table.

"I took the liberty of ordering wine for the table," Lance says once I have thanked the escort, and he has moved away. "I hope that's alright?"

"Of course, thank you," I say.

After the initial pleasantries have been exchanged a waiter appears with three burgundy leather clad menus. He hands one to each of us and we each thank him. Alex and I open our menus. Lance puts his straight down.

"I always order the same thing," he says. "Wild mushroom risotto followed by the roasted pheasant and chocolate fondant for dessert."

That answers a question I didn't want to have to ask about how many courses we are having. I didn't want to order three courses and have Lance and Alex only order mains or vice versa.

I scan through the menu, all of which looks delicious. Finally, I choose a lobster ravioli for starters, a filet mignon for main and vanilla and lime cheesecake for dessert.

I put my menu down, my decision made. Alex is still looking but he isn't much longer than I was. The waiter returns the instant he puts the menu down. I have to admit the wait staff in these types of places are usually very good and this man is no exception. Lance orders his dishes and I order mine. Alex orders last. He chooses the risotto, followed by the halibut and he also opts for the cheesecake for dessert. The waiter types it all into his tablet and then moves away and the sommelier takes his place, making a grand show of opening the wine Lance has ordered.

He pours a tiny bit into a glass which Lance swills around, sniffs and then tastes, nodding his approval.

"When our main courses arrive, please see that we have a good matching wine each," Lance says. He glances at Alex and then me. "Our sommelier here is very good. Are you happy to go with his selections?"

We both say yes, and I imagine how awkward it would have been if one of us had said no, especially if it was me with my lack of wine knowledge when I then went on to order the house special or something equally bad.

The first lot of wine is poured and then our appetizers are brought out. I've never felt so fussed over for a meal in my life and while the constant attention from the staff isn't bothering me tonight, it would drive me mad if this was a social occasion and I wanted to chat with my friends. Finally, with instructions to enjoy our food, we're left alone with our starters.

They are presented beautifully, and a little taste tells me they taste every bit as good as they look. It's all I can do not to moan in pleasure as I try mine.

"Beautiful as always," Lance says. "Alex? What do you think?"

"It's lovely," he replies.

"And you Ros? I've never actually tried the ravioli," Lance says.

"It's really good. The best I've had," I say honestly which earns me a beaming smile from Lance.

"So, then Lance, what brings us here tonight?" Alex asks.

Lance waves his hand dismissively at Alex.

"Let's not talk business while we eat. We aren't cavemen after all. There will be plenty of time to discuss everything after the meal," he says.

So, this isn't going to be a quick bite and home for nine o'clock then. It sounds like Lance has every intention of making it an all-night thing. If I had known that in advance, I would have been pissed off, but now I'm here, I don't find the idea so bad. I have two men – one of whom is as gorgeous as ever - being attentive to me, waiters to look after my every need, and delicious food and excellent wine. I'm not going to pretend it couldn't be a lot worse than this.

Our empty appetizer dishes are cleared away and the main courses arrive. I cut into my steak, and it is cooked to a perfect medium rare, just how I like it. We all comment on how good the food is and how well the chosen wines match each dish, and we pretty much repeat the same comments when first the waiter and then the sommelier drop by our table to check that everything is to our liking.

Alex and Lance chat as we eat. I mostly listen, laughing at some of their stories and chiming in when I have something relevant to add. It's a pleasant evening and the more I'm drinking, the more I'm relaxing and actually starting to enjoy myself.

I finish my main course and despite being pretty much full, I could happily eat it again, it was that good. I excuse myself to go to the bathroom, and Lance points me in the right direction. I use the bathroom and as I make my way back to the table, I see Will sitting alone at the bar in the dining area. I feel bad for him, and I go over to him. It's probably not my place to ask him to join us, but it won't hurt to chat with him for a bit.

"Hi," I say as I approach him.

"Hello," he replies.

Even as he answers me, his eyes are all over the room, checking everything and everyone constantly.

"Doesn't it bother you sitting here alone like this?" I ask.

Will shakes his head.

"No. It's my job," he says. "The whole point is to fade into the background so I'm not memorable. And while this is a social occasion for Alex, for me, it's just work."

I think about this for a moment, and it actually makes

perfect sense. It's not like Will is on a night out with his friends and they have ditched him. He is working and his job just happens to be tailing someone who at this moment is in a restaurant.

"That makes sense. Sorry to have bothered you," I say.

"You haven't bothered me, I just wanted you to know I'm not some sad little hermit in my actual life," Will says and he smiles at me. His smile changes his stoic face to a warm, friendly expression that I didn't think Will was capable of wearing.

I smile back and head back to the table where our desserts are just arriving. My cheesecake is amazing. The base is a ginger biscuit rather than the standard graham cracker and then there is a luxurious layer of vanilla cream cheese and the whole thing is topped with a zesty lime sauce. I'm more than stuffed when I finish it, but again, I would kill for another helping.

Our waiter comes over and asks us if we would like any coffees. We all look at each other and shake our heads.

"No thank you," Lance says. "But could we get three brandies brought to our table in the lounge please?"

"Of course, sir," the waiter says.

"Shall we?" Lance says and Alex and I stand up.

Lance follows suit and we follow him through the dining room, across the entrance way and into the bar at the other side of the room. I glance over my shoulder and see Will dutifully following us and sitting at the bar in the new room as we take our places at a secluded table toward the back of the room. The brandies come as we are seated and Lance makes a toast, holding his glass up.

"To a long and happy working relationship," he says.

Alex and I raise our glasses and repeat his toast and then we all drink. The brandy is strong but smooth and it cuts a warming path down my insides as I swallow it.

"I guess the time has come to talk business," Lance says.

Alex and I exchange a look and nod. I've had a few glasses of wine, but I still feel like I'm sober and ready for work. After this brandy, I'm not so sure that will still be the case though, so I place the glass on the table. I'll wait until the discussion is over to drink the rest.

"I have recently acquired a new branch to my company. I've bought out the company formerly known as Managhan and Harrison. That includes all their retail stores, all of their online stores and a few other bits and pieces," Lance says.

I try my best to remain professional, but I can't help but show my shock. Managhan and Harrison is a huge company, big enough to rival the likes of Walmart. If my quick math in my head is even close to correct, then this will double our business with Lance, who is now smiling at me.

"I see you are a step ahead Ros," he says. "You've worked out that this is going to double my business with your firm, haven't you?"

I nod. There's no point in denying it. He doesn't seem to be offended by my reaction. He just smiles at me and then he goes on.

"Obviously to bring that level of business your way, I will need some guarantees," Lance says to Alex.

"Go on," Alex says.

"My current accountant. I want her working on this side of my business too. I'm not going to be a dick and ask for her to be exclusive to my account, but I do want the same person handling it all, and if I want to speak to her, I expect to be able to speak to her whenever I want to within reason," Lance says.

"Consider it done," Alex says. "Anything else?"

"I expect you to take my calls any time I call," Lance says. "Even if it's three am. Obviously I would only ever call at a time like that in a dire emergency."

"Agreed," Alex says.

"That's about it really," Lance says. "When I came in for the meeting the other week, it made me remember that the company really does have a personal touch and they do want to look after me. Do you think any of these massive faceless corporations would ask after my wife and kids? Of course they wouldn't. To them, I would just be an account number. I like that you are different."

"You'll always get a personal service from us Lance," I put in because he is looking at me now.

"Then I think all that's left to do is to sign the paperwork," he says.

He catches the eye of a passing waiter who comes over to our table. Lance hands him a small key.

"My briefcase is in locker fifteen. Can you get it for me please? And can we have three large brandies too please," he says.

"Of course, sir," the waiter says.

CHAPTER
Eight
ROS

He takes the key and heads to the bar where he speaks to the bartender, presumably passing on the drinks order. He leaves the room after that, and I turn my attention back to my three quarters full first brandy. I had better get that down if another one is on the way. I guess if I get a bit tipsy now, it doesn't matter that much because it seems the discussion is done.

I pick my glass up and pour my drink into my mouth. I wince as I swallow the brandy and cough a little bit as it burns my throat.

"Are you ok?" Lance asks me.

"Jeez Ros, that's good stuff, it's not the kind of drink you do a shot with," Alex says at the same time.

"I'm fine thanks," I say to Lance, forcing a smile. "It just caught in my throat, that's all."

I ignore Alex's comment, but I do give him a dirty look that makes him laugh softly.

Our new drinks arrive and then the waiter brings Lance's briefcase. He opens it and pulls out two copies of a contract and hands one to Alex and one to me.

"They're both the same. I just thought it would be quicker if you could both look through it at the same time," Lance says.

I read through the contract. It is a pretty standard contract, and I flick to the small print. There is nothing there to trip us up and if it was up to me, I would happily sign it. I smile up at Lance and push my copy of the contract back toward him.

"It all seems to be in order," I say.

Alex hasn't quite finished reading yet, but he is only a moment or two behind me.

"I agree," he says.

Lance calls the waiter back over and asks him to witness the signing of the document alongside me. The waiter agrees.

Lance hands Alex a pen and he signs the contract. Lance signs his name too. The waiter and I both sign to say we witnessed the signatures and then Lance thanks the waiter, who leaves our table, and he puts the paperwork back away in his briefcase. Finally, he raises his glass.

"To Brannigan's and Waters' Financial Enterprises having a long and strong working relationship," he says.

"Cheers," Alex and I say, and we all take a drink.

I brace myself for the coughing fit, but it doesn't come and as much as I hate to admit it, even to myself, Alex was right. It's the sort of drink you sip and savor, not one you swallow in one mouthful.

Lance finishes his drink and looks at his watch. He stands up.

"Alex, Ros, it's been a pleasure, but I really must go. I'm sorry to dash off like this, but you two feel free to stay as long as you like. My tab is still open," Lance says.

Alex and I stand up and we both shake Lance's hand and say our goodbyes. We watch him until he's out of the room and then we look at each other and grin.

"I can't believe that just happened," Alex says.

"Me neither," I say.

"Julie's workload is going to double with this account, so I think I'll have to look into hiring another accountant, maybe even two," Alex says.

"I think that would be a good idea," I agree.

"Thanks for being here tonight, Ros. Lance really likes you being present, and I think you joining us probably sealed the deal," Alex says.

I'm shocked that he has said something so complimentary to me and I'm even more shocked when he puts his hand over mine where it rests on the table. He gives it a gentle squeeze. I think that is the first time we have touched since we shook hands when we first met, and the shock waves that dance through my skin at his touch almost take my breath away. It seems to affect him the same way and for a second, his hand sits on mine, and we look into each other's eyes. It feels like the bar around us has melted away leaving just Alex and me floating in our own little world.

The sound of the door to the bar opening and then closing again breaks the spell and suddenly I'm flustered, and Alex seems to be the same. We both pull our hands away from each other and I jump to my feet.

"I'm just going to the bathroom," I say.

"I'll call us a car, should I?" Alex says.

I nod and practically run from him to the ladies' room. I go to the sinks and look in the mirror above them. My skin is pleasantly flushed, and I don't know if it's from the brandy or if it's from Alex's touch, but I do know that no one has ever given me a reaction like that just from touching my hand. Imagine what it would feel like to have him touching other parts of my body. My pussy is wet and ready for him, but I ignore the longing in my body and remind myself that this is Alex we're talking about here. Alex, who is a dick. The same Alex who was cold to me for so long and only warmed up to me slightly when he saw that I was important to his biggest client.

I shake my head and go and use the toilet and then I come back and wash my hands. When I can't think of anything else to do to waste time, I leave the room and go back to our table. Alex has his back to the bathroom door, and it gives me another moment to prepare myself to be in his line of sight. He looks up as I reach the table and I smile at him, trying my best to appear normal.

"Did you manage to get us a ride?" I ask.

"Yeah. It'll be here in five minutes," Alex says, and he too looks like he's trying to be normal now, and I figure it's best just not to think about that moment when we touched and the way it made me feel.

We finish our drinks, and while I'm tempted to gulp what's left of mine, I remember my reaction to that, and I sip it slowly instead. By the time I've finished, I think the car must be about due.

"Ready?" Alex asks me as his cell phone beeps.

I nod, assuming the beep was a notification telling him our car is outside. We both stand up and I follow Alex, but instead of heading straight for the door, he veers toward the bar and speaks to Will first.

"My car is outside, and I am only going straight home," he says. "Consider yourself off duty."

"Thanks" Will says, patting Alex on the shoulder. "See you later then."

Alex and I leave the bar and exit the building. A car the same as the one that collected me earlier waits for us.

"I thought we could share. Your place is on the way to mine. I hope that's ok," Alex says.

"It's fine," I say.

I almost demand to know how he knows where I live, but then I remember he had me picked up to get here and I gave him the address so that he could. I really think that last brandy has gone to my head. I need to be careful what I say now.

The driver opens the door for us, and I get in first and slide over. Alex follows me and the driver closes the door. We set off and Alex speaks up.

"Can you stop by the office please Mike?" he says. "I just need to grab something."

"No problem," the driver replies.

We aren't that far from the office and the driver soon pulls up outside of the building. Alex starts to get out but then he turns back to me.

"Do you want to come up for a quick drink to celebrate where we don't have to act all demure because we're in public," he asks.

CHAPTER
Nine

ROS

"Yeah, sure, why not," I agree.

"Just drop us here Mike. I'll call back when we're ready to go," Alex says, and we get out of the car and go into the office building.

It's not that late – it's only eleven o'clock, but the building is deserted and silent. Being with Alex makes it ok, but I think if I was alone, I would find it extremely creepy. We get into the elevator and Alex hits the button for our floor.

"It's so quiet," I say. "It's weird."

"You've obviously never worked late before huh?" Alex says.

"Obviously I have," I reply. "But generally speaking, when that happened, there was something big on the go and I wouldn't be the only one working. Half of the office would still be here, and it would just feel the same as it does in the daytime."

"I was joking Ros," Alex says. "Lighten up a little, would you?"

I guess for a moment there I thought he was going back to

his old ways where he would berate me about anything and everything at any given opportunity.

"Oh. Sorry," I mumble. "I just thought that…"

"That I had gone back to being an absolute douchebag to you," Alex finishes for me.

I nod, feeling my eyes widen in surprise to hear him admit to it.

"I know I wasn't exactly fair to you when I first started here," he says.

I shrug. "I wasn't exactly welcoming either. Let's just leave the past in the past."

The elevator pings open on our floor, and we step out and head toward Alex's office.

"I actually think we make a pretty good team, you and me," Alex says.

"Yes, I agree," I say.

We go into the office and Alex goes to the drink's cabinet in the corner.

"Is vodka ok?" he asks me, and I nod.

"I have coke or tonic," he says.

"Tonic please," I say.

I watch as he makes the drinks and then he hands me one and gestures for me to sit down on the couch below the window. I do and he sits beside me. He clinks his glass against mine.

"To us and to the biggest contract this company has ever seen," he says.

"And to moving forward as a good team," I add.

We both sip our drinks, but Alex seems to have deflated, and he looks down into his lap.

"What is it?" I ask.

He shakes his head.

"It's nothing," he says.

"It's clearly something," I press him.

He sighs and glances at me.

"Ok. But if I tell you, you have to promise me that you won't quit the firm," he says.

That sounds awfully ominous and suddenly it doesn't feel like we're celebrating anymore. I put my glass down on the ground beside my feet.

"Go on," I say.

"Promise me first," Alex insists.

"I promise," I say.

Really, what can he say that would be bad enough that I would leave my job; a job I had stuck with even when he was at his worst? And, if it is something I can't get past, he can't really stop me from resigning just because I had said I wouldn't do it. People change their mind about shit like that all the time after all.

"In the interest of moving forward as a team, I will tell you something I never imagined myself telling anyone, least of all you. Do you remember when I first started at the company, and you were making a lot of silly mistakes with figures and what not?" Alex says. It's a question but he doesn't pause for me to answer him, and I don't attempt to interrupt him to tell him that yes, of course I remember, and those errors weren't mine. "You didn't make those mistakes Ros. I was sabotaging you."

Well, I did not see that coming.

"What?" I demand. "Why?"

"I wanted Celia as my assistant and the only way I could achieve that was to get rid of you. But because of my grandfather's clause, I had to have a good reason for getting rid of you so, I decided to create a chain of errors that no reasonable person could insist I overlook," he replies. "It wasn't personal and now I'm so glad it didn't work."

I feel anger smash through me. How could he do that to me? And how could he risk the client's accounts like that.

Although I suppose he knew what he had done where and was able to fix it before any clients saw the damage he had done. Or had they? What about Lance Donovan?

"That's why there was a mistake in Lance's accounts isn't it?" I ask.

"Yes," Alex says and at least he has the decency to look a bit sheepish. "I know how close it came to blowing up in my face, but at the same time, it worked out well because that was when you really came into your own. You swooped in and saved that account like it was nothing and I knew Celia would never be able to pull that kind of thing off. For what it's worth, I am really sorry, and your job is safe."

"You are a total fucking asshole," I say.

I debate telling him I blamed Celia for sabotaging me, but he's saying something else and the moment for me to do so passes.

"But you'll forgive me though, right?" he says.

"Why should I?" I demand.

"Because I'm sorry. Because you want to. Because it's the easiest route forward," Alex says. "Take your pick."

He's moved closer to me on the couch as he's talking and I realize I can feel the heat from his thigh on mine, and our bodies are less than an inch from touching. I guess coming clean and then getting moaned at is turning Alex on. And that thought is turning me on. My pussy is damp, and I want nothing more than Alex filling it up.

I ignore the feeling in my pussy and think about whether or not I should forgive Alex. I suppose I'll have to at some point, and it might as well be now. It'll keep the peace and make working together a lot easier.

"I suppose I might be able to forgive you," I say.

Alex turns to look at me and I feel myself moving forward as he does. We sit, our faces inches from each other's.

"I was a bad boy," Alex says.

It should be cheesy, him delivering a line like that, but it isn't. Instead of making me laugh, I feel like I would have assumed what I would do if someone had asked me what my reaction would be in this situation, it makes me more turned on and I can't help but play along.

"Well then, you had better be on your best behavior from now on," I say.

"Ah come on. Every woman loves a bad boy," Alex says.

He is so close to me now that I can feel his breath tickling my lips when he talks.

"Not me," I say.

"Oh?" Alex says, sounding surprised. "So then why are you kissing me?"

He presses his lips against mine the second he stops talking and I have another rush of warm wetness from my pulsing pussy.

The kiss starts out gentle, almost chaste, but after a second or two, it's like we have been unleashed. Our mouths open and our tongues hungrily swirl in each other's mouths. Our hands roam over each other's bodies and after a second, I push myself up from the couch without taking my lips away from Alex's and I straddle his lap. His hands cup my ass and I push my hands into his hair.

Alex pulls his tongue from my mouth and kisses down my neck. I move my head to the side, giving him easier access to the tender skin there, skin that tingles at his kiss. He works on my neck, his hands moving up and down my back and my pussy is going mad with desire. I can't wait to feel him filling me up. He nips my skin gently between his teeth and I moan. He pulls back and smiles up at me. I smile at him and then I reach for his tie. I loosen it and pull it over his head and throw it on the couch beside us.

I lean down and run my lips over Alex's lips, and we kiss again, deeper and even more passionate than the last one. I open the top button of his shirt and I'm moving on to the next one when I hear voices outside of the office door. Alex and I come apart and frown at each other and then the office door is opening, and I jump from Alex's lap as though he has become poisonous. By the time the door opens all the way, we are sitting side by side once more. We probably both look a little bit worse for wear, but it's not obvious we were on the verge of fucking each other's brains out.

As the woman in the doorway registers that we are there, her face looks as shocked as I feel. I realize from the vacuum cleaner in her hand and the overalls she's wearing, that she's a cleaner and another one is right behind her.

"Oh, I'm so sorry," she says. "I didn't know you were still here. I'll come back."

"No, no it's fine," Alex says, smiling at the woman. "There's no need to apologize."

"Yes, come on in and do what you need to do. I was just leaving anyway," I say.

I jump up from the couch. Now that the spell between Alex and me has been broken, I can hardly wait to get out of here. I can't believe how close I came to fucking him. Especially after his confession and us finally reaching a place where we can work together without any issues between us. Talk about almost swapping one problem for another one.

"See you tomorrow," I say to Alex as I grab my purse and head for his office door.

The cleaners have moved into the office and Alex follows me to the door, letting them get on with their work in peace.

"Wait Ros," he says. "Just let me grab my jacket and I'll call us a car."

"No, it's ok," I say, knowing if I'm alone with him again, it will be too hard for me to resist finishing what we started. "I'll get a cab or something."

"Ros…" Alex starts.

"Goodnight Alex," I say, and turn and walk away, leaving him in a position where he can't really come after me without raising the suspicion of the cleaners.

I hurry from the building and when I step outside, I take a second to breath in a few deep lungs full of the cool night air, and then I start to walk toward home, watching for a cab I can flag down as I go.

CHAPTER Ten

ALEX

"Come in," I call when there's a knock on my office door.

The door opens and Ros comes in.

"You wanted to see me?" she says.

Always, I think to myself. Instead of answering Ros with words, I stand up and beckon for her to come closer. She does, a puzzled expression on her face. Her puzzlement changes to desire when I meet her halfway across the office and pull her against me, my lips mashing against hers. Our lips meld as one, moving together as our tongues move into each other's mouths and we taste each other. As we kiss, our hands roam frantically over each other's bodies, tugging at each other's clothes and caressing the skin beneath them. Within moments, we are naked, our clothes scattered on the ground around us.

I run my lips along Ros's bare collar bone, tasting the salty sweetness of her skin. As I do, I run my already hard cock through her slit, feeling how wet she is for me. I can't wait any longer and I spin her around and bend her over my desk.

I take in the sight of her bare ass, her glistening pussy, and I line my cock up, ready to push inside of her.

A knock on my office door pulls me out of my fantasy. I can't help but keep on thinking about the kiss Ros and I shared last night in this very office, and what might have happened after it if the damned cleaners hadn't arrived when they did. I was hoping to see Ros first thing when I came in, before many other people were in so we could maybe finish what we started, but when I came into my office, Ros's desk was empty, and my own dirty mind had to be enough to keep me company until now.

"Fuck," I say underneath my breath. I wait for a moment until my cock goes down and then in what I hope is a normal voice, I answer the knock. "Come in."

The door opens and Celia comes in. It's my own fault I was disturbed in the middle of my deepest fantasy because I asked one of the other receptionists to have Celia come and see me as soon as she got in this morning. Fuck. I hate how efficient the reception staff are.

"Good morning," I say, forcing myself to smile and reminding myself it's not Celia's fault she interrupted me. "Come on in and sit down. I need to talk to you about something."

Celia turns around and closes the door and then comes and sits down at my desk opposite me.

"Is everything ok?" Celia asks.

"Yes, everything is fine," I say. "I just wanted to tell you to your face that I am no longer considering you for the position of my assistant."

"What?" Celia shouts. I was expecting an angry reaction, and she doesn't disappoint me. "Is this some sort of a fucking joke Alex, because it's not funny at all?"

"It's not a joke Celia. Not at all," I reply, making sure I stay calm because I don't want this to turn into a slanging match. I just want to inform Celia of my decision and have her go away and brood on it somewhere else. "Because of the circumstances where I asked you to come with me to this firm, I am willing to continue paying you at your current rate if you would like to stay on as a receptionist, which I have to say you're doing a great job of."

"Now you're just being fucking sarcastic," Celia snaps. "It's not like the job is exactly hard, is it?"

"So then be grateful you're doing something you find easy for the wages of a much harder job," I say.

"I just don't get it," Celia says. "At least tell me what I did to make you change your mind. And don't say it's because I'm good at reception. You could find another receptionist easily and we both know it."

"It's not anything you did wrong," I reassure her. "My decision is based on having seen Ros in the role for a while now, I've realized she's actually a very good assistant and she doesn't deserve to lose her job."

"Oh, you've got to be fucking kidding me," Celia snaps.

"Not at all," I say again. "You know how much I wanted you to have this job. I even tried to sabotage Ros myself so that I had an excuse to fire her, but she kept rising to the top despite that and I realized I'd have to be an idiot to let her go."

Celia is quiet for a moment, and she glares at me and then slowly, her facial expression turns into a knowing smile.

"You fucking like her don't you?" she says.

"Don't go there," I say.

"You're not denying it I notice," Celia says.

"I don't like Ros," I say. "And even if I did, that would have no bearing on whether or not she could do the job."

"I can't decide if you're in denial or if you're just lying to me, but either way, she's got my job because you like her. It's obvious," Celia says, and she smirks at me.

"That's enough Celia. I'm still your boss and you need to watch your lip," I say.

Celia doesn't respond, although judging by the angry expression on her face, there are plenty of things she wants to say to me. I don't have the time to sit and argue with Celia all day and even if I did have the time to do it, I don't want to. I've said what I needed to say, and she can either accept it and stay on as a receptionist or she can decide to not accept it and leave. I'd like her to stay, but if she chooses not to, she wasn't wrong about me being able to replace her on reception easily enough so I'm not too worried about keeping her sweet.

"That will be all," I say.

Celia raises an eyebrow and shakes her head at me, but she gets up and leaves my office and I let the sheer cheek of her go. Honestly, that woman is getting above her station and the only reason I let her get away with her insubordination today is because I do feel kind of bad asking her to come here to be my assistant and then changing my mind on her. But that's business. And that's all it is. This decision has nothing to do with how I feel about Ros.

Or at least I hope it doesn't. No, scratch that thought. I know it doesn't. I made the decision to keep Ros on as my assistant ages before anything happened between us. Hell, the kiss we shared only happened because of my confession and her anger about it turned me on enough that I just had to kiss her.

It does tell me something though. If Celia, who I have worked with for years and who I think of as a friend too, thinks my decisions are clouded by my feelings for someone, it says everyone in the office will and I don't want my decision to be constantly questioned. Probably no one but Celia would dare question me to my face, but that doesn't change the fact there will be whispers and if staff starts thinking something is unfair, they are more likely to be unhappy which makes them care less about the job and therefore be more likely to make mistakes.

I refuse to be the subject of office gossip, and this is a good reminder of why I have always had a rule about not mixing business and pleasure. As much as I want to kiss Ros again and do a whole lot more to her, I'm going to have to control myself, because from now on, Ros and I can only have a professional relationship. I need to force myself to only see her as an employee and make sure that I don't treat her any better than I treat any of my staff.

CHAPTER
Eleven

ROS

I look up from my desk at the sound of Alex's office door opening. I expect to see Alex coming out of the room, but instead, I see Celia exiting. She's walking perfectly normally until she sees me looking in her direction, and then she starts to tug at her clothes and pat her hair as though she's putting herself right after a make out session. I just roll my eyes. I don't know why she thinks I would fall for that, and even if I did, I don't know why she thinks I would let her see that it bothered me.

She changes direction slightly and makes a beeline for my desk. I smile at her, although I would rather scratch her eyes out than be nice to her.

"Good morning, Celia," I say.

"You fucking little bitch," she replies. Not the response I was expecting, I have to be honest. "You sit there all innocent and sweet, saying good morning to me, knowing fine well you have taken my job."

"Taken your job?" I say with a soft laugh. "I don't think so. This has been my job for the last three years. You mistakenly assumed you could come in and take it, but that doesn't make it yours."

"Maybe I should sleep with Alex and then I would get whatever I wanted from him like you do," she says.

"I was under the impression the way you came out of his office tugging at your clothes that you wanted me to believe you were sleeping with him," I say.

"Dammit," Celia curses.

I swear I hear a snort of laughter from Will's direction, but when I look over there, he has a straight face, and he isn't even looking in our direction.

"Ugh. Why can't you just…" Celia starts, and I wait for the stinging insult that is to follow it.

Something like curl up and die is my guess as to what's coming. Or maybe something more basic like just fuck off. But before Celia can finish her thought, Alex's office door opens again, and this time, Alex himself steps out into the hallway. It's comical to see the change in Celia. She goes from being partially bent down to really get into my face, her face screwed up in anger, to standing normally, and smiling down at me.

"Give someone else some of your tasks to do and get an early finish for once? You do far too much," she finishes up for Alex's benefit.

Great. Not only does she sound like a sweet and concerned colleague, but she has also managed to make it sound like I was complaining about my workload.

"Don't be silly," I say, a smile as fake as Celia's plastered onto my face. "You've done the assistant's job yourself at your last company. You know as well as I do that outsourcing any of your tasks just means you have to redo them later."

"That's true," Celia says with a fake little laugh. "Well, I'd best dash. Catch you later Ros."

"Nice talking to you," I reply.

I check Alex isn't within hearing distance before I mutter "two faced bitch" under my breath. This time, there is no doubting that Will laughs, and I look up quickly enough to see him still laughing and I laugh with him.

I go back to focusing on my work. I need to have a word with Alex, but I'm not sure if he has gone to the kitchen or the bathroom and I really don't want to be someone who stalks her boss at the bathroom. I just want to apologize to him for the way I ran off last night. It can definitely wait until he comes back to his office.

When he does come back along, I'm talking on the telephone, and I have to wait until I've finished the conversation. As soon as I have, I get up out of my chair and go and knock on Alex's office door. I open it when he calls out for me to come inside, and I do as he says, stepping in and closing the door with a quiet clicking sound behind me.

"Have you got a minute please?" I ask.

"Sure," Alex says. "Come and sit down. Is everything ok?"

I nod as I move toward the offered seat opposite Alex. I sit down.

"I just wanted to apologize to you about last night," I say, feeling the blood rushing to my cheeks and making me look flushed. "The way I ran out on you after we kissed, I mean."

"You don't have to apologize, Ros. If anything, I should be apologizing to you." Alex says.

I wave his words away. What does he have to apologize for? He didn't run away from me like some kid who has their first kiss and panics.

"I just... the thought of how close we came to getting caught," I say.

"Yes, the idea of being seen with me must be awful," Alex says.

I roll my eyes.

"That's not what I meant at all, and you know it," I say. "You must know what the gossip would be like. The assistant shagging the boss, and every achievement I have being questioned, every good thing that happens to me getting a side whisper of it's because she's shagging her boss. I've always said I would never cross the line between working for someone and having something happen between us. It caught me by surprise when I allowed it to happen, that's all."

"Don't worry about any gossip," Alex says. "What happened between us was stupid and unprofessional and it won't happen again, so there's no danger of anyone talking about it."

So, it was just a drunken mistake to Alex then, which explains why he doesn't care that I ran out on him. He obviously decided that made it easier for him because we were on the same page. Bastard.

"If there's nothing else, I do have some calls to make," Alex says, and I realize I'm being dismissed. It is the final insult and I get up and turn away quickly, the sting of tears in my eyes. I leave Alex's office without a word and go straight to the ladies' room.

I refuse to allow myself to cry. Partly because I don't have any makeup with me to fix my face after a crying session and partly because that bastard doesn't deserve my tears. I know rationally he basically said the same thing as I was thinking about crossing the line between personal and professional, but he said it in such a cold way, a way that said kissing me was a mistake because of way more than crossing a professional line.

I take a deep breath and wash my hands and then I exit the bathroom and go back to my desk. I won't give Alex any reasons to have a go at me, not when I feel like I could cry at any moment. I will throw myself into my work and try to avoid contact with him where possible.

This seems to work for me until just before lunch when Alex opens his office door.

"Ros, get in here," he shouts.

What a lovely way to talk to me, I think to myself, rolling my eyes, but I'm not in the mood to argue with him, so I just get up and go to his office. By the time I get there, he's back behind his desk, and I stand in the middle of the office looking at him, waiting to see what the hell he wants now.

"I asked you to have the Merriman file on my desk before lunch time," he says.

"Right," I say.

"Don't get cocky Ros. Where the fuck is it?" Alex demands.

"On your desk like you asked for it to be," I say. I walk forward a couple of steps until I'm at Alex's desk, and I lift up a few papers and point to the Merriman file on his desk where I left it. "Are you back to sabotaging me Alex?"

"No, of course not," he says dismissively. "You know I like things in their rightful places and files for my attention go here."

He points at the usual space he has cleared for files, but today, the space is taken up by a pile of papers.

"I thought those might be important and I didn't want to mess them up," I say.

"That's not for you to decide," Alex says. "Put things where you are told to in the future."

"And then you can call me in and have a go because I covered up something important you were working on," I say. "It seems to me that you just wanted an excuse to call me in here."

Alex glares at me and I look back at him, careful to keep my face neutral.

"Maybe you put the file there on purpose so I would have no choice but to call you in," he says.

"I honestly didn't think you were that petty," I say, and I mean it.

I wonder if this had happened before the kiss and the subsequent conversation if he still would have called me in to moan about the placement of a file. Something tells me he wouldn't have.

"While you're here, you might as well make yourself useful. I have a lunch time call, so I'll be eating my lunch in my office today. Go out to that deli across the street and get me a ham salad sandwich and a packet of salt and vinegar chips please. Oh, and a can of orange soda," Alex says.

"Ok," I say through gritted teeth. "I'll get right on that."

"And see if Will wants anything. He won't be leaving for lunch if I'm not," Alex says.

I nod, not trusting my voice to come out steady. I don't want Alex to see how angry I am. He has obviously given me this task to anger me, and I won't give him the satisfaction of seeing it has worked. This is the sort of task given to work experience kids, not personal assistants, but I know technically, my job is pretty much to do whatever Alex tells me to do and that could include a personal errand. Hell, I know some personal assistants who have to pick up their boss's dry cleaning and do their grocery shopping. Grabbing lunch for Alex really is nothing compared to that, especially when he has a meeting over lunch time.

Alex grabs his wallet out of his pocket and hands me a twenty-dollar bill. I take it and stand up to leave the office. Alex doesn't seem to have anything else to say to me and that suits me just fine. I leave the room, careful not to slam the door and give him the satisfaction of knowing I have been biting my tongue in there.

I go to my desk and grab my purse. I debate just storming off and not bothering to check in with Will, but I remind myself this isn't his fault and it's not fair he should go hungry because Alex is an ass. I approach Will.

"I'm popping out to get Alex's lunch because he won't be leaving the office today," I say. "He said to see if you want me to get you anything while I'm out. I'm going to that deli place across the street."

"Would you mind?" Will says. "I feel awful having you go on an errand for me, but as you said, I can't leave if Alex isn't, and I didn't have any breakfast this morning."

"I don't mind at all," I say, and I mean it. To be honest, I wouldn't have minded getting Alex his lunch if he had asked nicely instead of demanding it, and Will at least has the decency to look like this is making him feel a bit awkward.

"Can you grab me a roast beef on rye please," he says. "No salad. And a bottle of water."

"Sure," I say. "I won't be long."

"Wait. You need some money," Will says.

I shake my head and pat my pocket where Alex's twenty dollars sits.

"This one's on Alex," I say.

I don't actually know if I was meant to pay for Will's lunch from Alex's money or whether I was meant to get Will's own money from him, but fuck it, I'm doing it this way and if Alex isn't happy about it, he can suck it up or go and ask Will for the money back himself.

I go to the deli and get Alex and Will their lunches with Alex's money and while I'm there, I pick myself up a chicken and bacon mayo sandwich with my own money, and then I head back to the office. I put our lunches away in the kitchen and then I sit down at my desk and get on with my work.

CHAPTER
Twelve

ROS

I'm glad when it's finally time for me to finish work. Generally speaking, I love my job, and while I like it being quitting time, I don't count the minutes to it like I have today. Today though, Alex has been an absolute dick to me all day. He's made several unreasonable requests and gotten even more snarky when I've explained why those requests were unreasonable. I mean he must know they were crazy – one of his requests was that I computerize two years' worth of archived accounts in three hours. He has also given me a few more menial tasks like picking up his dry cleaning. I get that for most people, that is part of the personal assistant's role, but Mr. Waters never used me for personal errands and Alex never has before today; it's just not good value for money sending me to do those things at my rate when we have interns who can do it for much less. It's like I brought it on myself by thinking about it earlier. Maybe I should think about Alex being nice to me.

I was going to let it go, simply because I don't want Alex to know his little game has worked and that he's gotten underneath my skin, but enough is enough, and if I don't say anything, he might actually think it's ok to treat me this way and continue on with it. Fuck that.

I'm all caught up and ready to leave, my jacket on and my purse in my hand, but I turn toward Alex's office instead of the elevators and I go and tap on the door. He calls for me to come in and I do, closing the door behind me.

"You know earlier when you said you kissing me was a stupid and unprofessional mistake?" I ask. Alex looks up from his work and nods his head. He keeps on looking at me, waiting for me to go on. "Well, I just want you to know that being a dick to someone because you kissed them is also stupid and unprofessional and I expect from tomorrow, that you start to treat me with a little bit of respect once more. I am your assistant, not your errand girl."

I've said way more than I meant to, and I wait for Alex to get angry with me, but instead, he looks at me, a smirk of amusement on his lips. That smirk is way more annoying than if he had been angry. What the fuck was amusing about what I have just said to him?

"Noted," he says, and his voice also relays his amusement.

I want to argue with him, to tell him not to laugh at me, but I will only get angrier and if he keeps smirking at me like that, I know I'll cross the line and say something I will regret, so I just turn around and leave the office without another word, and this time, I make sure that I do slam the door. I'm sure I can hear Alex laughing inside his office as I walk away, but I'm not sure enough to go back and give him another piece of my mind, so I keep walking and ignore the sound.

I drive home and when I get there and enter my apartment, I'm still fuming with Alex and his smirking that wasn't sexy at all – not even a little bit.

"He is so freaking annoying," I say to Fiona as I throw myself into my armchair.

Fiona is laying on the couch watching TV, which she mutes and then looks at me.

"Who?" she asks.

"Who do you think? Alex," I say.

"I thought he was treating you better now," Fiona says, sitting up and turning to face me with her legs crossed in front of her.

"He was. Until we kissed and then today, he has been an absolute dick again," I say.

"Wait. What? You guys kissed? You kept that quiet," Fiona says.

"This is the first time I've seen you since it happened. I got in late last night and you were already at work when I got up this morning," I say.

"Ok, I'll let you off the hook for now," Fiona says with a grin. "But now I want details."

"What do you mean details? We kissed. That's it," I say.

"Where were you? Who instigated the kiss? Was it a good kiss? Why did you stop kissing? Do you want to do it again? Just for starters," Fiona says.

I roll my eyes, but I answer her questions, ticking off each point on my finger as I answer.

"We were in Alex's office after the dinner with the client I told you about. Alex made the first move, but we were both being quite flirty and if he hadn't made it, I probably would have. Yes, it was a good kiss. We stopped kissing because the cleaners appeared. I did want to do it again, but not anymore," I tell her.

"Why not? What happened?" she asks.

"When we got interrupted, I kind of overreacted and ran from Alex. I apologized to him this morning for it, and he told me not to worry about it, that the kiss was unprofessional and a mistake. Now that stung, but I could have accepted it. But then all day he's been awful to me, almost as bad as he was when I first started working for him. I was just taking it and trying not to let him get to me, but then I thought no, why should he get away with talking to me like this? So, I went to his office and told him that acting like a dick because of a kiss was also unprofessional and a mistake. I don't know what I expected. An explanation. Maybe even an apology. Like I said, I don't know what I was expecting from him really. But he just smirked at me and said it was noted," I say. "I expected something… more, I guess."

"It kind of sounds like he's playing some sort of a game with you. Like seeing how mean he can be and still keep you on the hook – because for the record, going into his office and announcing that showed him you are still very much on the hook," Fiona says.

"I'm not still on his hook. I hate him," I say.

Fiona laughs and shakes her head,

"Bullshit," she says. "Look at you, all flustered because of him. You're gagging for him girl."

I sigh.

"Well maybe I'm not completely over him. But I don't let it show to him," I say.

"Except when you tell him he's being a dick because you kissed instead of just saying he's being a dick," Fiona says.

"Fuck," I say. "Now what the hell do I do?"

"Seduce him," Fiona says with a casual shrug as she's suggested nothing more than grabbing him a can of soda. "He's still into you. It's obvious."

"No, it's not obvious at all," I say. "I really don't think he's into me. But that's not what I meant anyway. Fi, I've had one relationship where I was messed up, and every day was a new head fucking game. I won't go there again. That relationship taught me that I am no one's punch bag, literally or verbally, and I won't let Alex play me."

Fiona thinks for a moment, and she nods her head.

"Ok," she says. "Here's what you do. You go in there and be Ros fucking Thomas and show the bastard that he isn't getting to you. Be cool and calm and ultra professional and let him see his little games aren't having any effect on you."

"I think I can do that," I say.

"Of course you can," Fiona says encouragingly. "And if you find yourself wanting to be flirty with him, or if you find yourself strangely attracted to that cocky little smirk that I just know this man does, then imagine he's a woman. If your boss was a woman and she was treating you badly, how would you act?"

"Exactly like you described. Cool, calm, professional," I say.

"So, there you go then. Act the part until it becomes second nature to you," Fiona says.

"I will," I say. I smile for what feels like the first time in a good few hours. "Thanks Fi. You always have the best advice."

CHAPTER
Thirteen

ALEX

"Well, I think that went quite well, don't you?" I say to Ros as we tuck into steaks and baked potatoes in a small restaurant across the street from our hotel.

Ros nods her head.

"Yes, definitely. I'd be surprised if we don't get a yes from them," she says.

We have just come from a two-hour long meeting with the board of directors of a decent sized company who are looking for new financial representation. We did a presentation and then we had a question-and-answer session with them and to be honest, although I don't want to get ahead of myself and jinx us, I feel pretty much the same way as Ros – I'll be surprised if we don't get a yes from them.

"You were right," I say. "It definitely made a difference coming to them rather than doing it over a video conference call. It made it feel more real and it was much easier to connect with them on a personal level."

Ros nods her head.

"I think technology has its place and it is invaluable for

some things, but when it comes to meeting people, I think you can't beat a face-to-face meeting. Video calls are great to go over any key points down the line once you have already made that connection," she says.

"And a night away and a meal on the company doesn't hurt either right," I say, flashing Ros a grin to show her I'm joking.

"I didn't say that," Ros laughs.

"But you were thinking it," I say also laughing.

"On that note, I'm pleading the fifth," she says.

"Cheat," I laugh and Ros grins back at me.

We eat in silence for a moment, and I see Ros looking over at Will where he sits with a clear line of vision to our table and to the door.

"You can't get used to Will always being here, can you?" I ask.

"It's not that," Ros says. "I always feel bad leaving him sitting alone. I know he prefers it that way, but it doesn't seem right."

"It's his preference and he gets very well compensated for his job," I say. "When I first hired him, I felt a lot like you do, but over time, I got used to the fact that he works how he works, and I started to let him call the shots with regards to where he would take up a seat and stuff like that. It's like with the setup at the hotel. I would have been happy to pay for three rooms, or a three-bedroom suite, but Will insisted that a two bedroom is fine because he wants to be in the living room regardless so he can be alert to anyone trying to get in."

"I wonder what he's like when he's not at work," Ros says. "Does he have a wife or children or anything?"

"No children or wife, but I'm sure he has girlfriends and people who he socializes with," I say.

"I bet he's the opposite of his professional persona. Like

he'll be the first one up and dancing at parties," Ros says with a giggle.

I can't imagine Will dancing, but I still laugh along with Ros.

"And he'd be the one talking constantly," I add.

Ros picks her glass up and lifts it up.

"To party Will," she says.

"To party Will," I repeat and we both drink.

We finish our meals and I push my plate away and sigh.

"I'm so stuffed," I say.

"Me too," Ros agrees. "I don't know about you, but I'm skipping dessert."

"Same," I say. "In fact, if you don't mind, I would kind of like to get back to the suite and get working on some of the things we've discussed today."

"That works for me," Ros says. "I have plenty of work I can be getting on with too."

I go to the bar and inform Will that we're leaving, and he jumps up from his stool and follows a few paces behind Ros and me as we head up to our suite. It's a lovely suite, comprising of a large living room which Will will be using as his sleeping quarters, a small kitchen, a master bathroom and two interconnecting bedrooms, each of which have their own ensuite toilet and shower room.

Ros and I both go into our respective bedrooms. I sit down on the bed and reach for my laptop, but then I decide to get comfortable first. I stand back up and remove my suit and shirt and tie, stripping naked, and I put my clothes on the small chair beneath the window, and then I go through to the shower room and get into the shower. I turn on the water and I'm greeted with a lovely power shower full of hot water. It feels so good on my skin that I just stand there for a few moments.

I can't help but think of Ros and how charming she was

today and tonight both with the client and afterward when there was only me and her. It's been over a week since we kissed and then she told me off for being a dick to her, which in hindsight, I realized she was right about. I made an effort to be nicer to her after that and it seemed that Ros did the same thing with me, and after a few days of frosty but civil interactions, we both seemed to relax a bit, and I would go as far as to say we are friendly toward each other now. The trouble is though, that's not enough for me. I want to be more than friends with Ros. But she made her feelings on that idea quite clear when she ran out on me after we kissed and then defended the action the next day. I need to accept that I can't have her.

Thinking about Ros while in the shower proves to be a mistake and I force myself to think of anything but her while I wash and rinse my hair and body, and by the time I shut the water off, my hard cock has gone back down. I brush my teeth and leave the bathroom. I don't bother wrapping a towel around me. The cool air feels nice on my naked body.

I step into the main bedroom from the en suite room at the exact same moment as Ros steps in from the adjoining door. She's taken off her work dress and jacket and she's wearing a thigh length t-shirt presumably as a nightgown. It has a kitten on it and a cute slogan about having a cat nap. Her hair is loose, and she has washed her makeup off. She looks so adorable that I just want to grab her and kiss her.

Her eyes widen when she sees that I'm naked and her cheeks flush dark red. My natural reaction is to cover my cock with my hands and dart back into the bathroom, but instead, I decide to brazen it out and I flash Ros a grin and saunter over to the chest of drawers. I pull open the top drawer and take out a pair of black boxer briefs. I put them on, my pace slow, and leisurely, like I often find women in my room when

I'm naked and casually dress in front of them without a care in the world.

"You are allowed to knock you know," I say when I straighten back up.

"I... I know. I'm sorry. I just thought you'd be working, I didn't expect..." She pauses and nods at my crotch. "Well... that."

I can't help but smile at her discomfort and she clears her throat and straightens up, trying to look less flustered.

"Well?" I ask. Ros just looks at me in confusion. "I assume you wanted something when you came in here?"

"Oh. Yes. I wanted to ask you something," she says.

"Go ahead," I say after a moment's pause.

"I forgot," Ros says, her cheeks flushing again.

I don't even try to hide my smile this time.

"Why don't you just admit that you wanted to see me naked?" I ask.

As I speak, I find myself moving closer to Ros, like my feet are drawing me to her.

"If that was the case, I would have just asked," Ros replies, and I realize that she too is moving forward, closing the gap between us.

"I would have said yes," I say.

"Then it's a shame you put the boxers on," Ros says, her voice a breathy whisper as she stops a foot away from me.

"They can come back off easily enough," I reply, and then we are on each other, our mouths pressing together, our hands roaming over each other's bodies.

I grab the bottom of Ros's t-shirt and lift it up. We break our kiss long enough for me to pull the t-shirt over her head and drop it on the ground and then we're back to kissing, but not before I notice that Ros is completely naked now. She pushes my boxer shorts down and I step out of them and kick them away. My cock is as hard as a rock once more and I moan as Ros's hand circles it and begins to move up and down my length.

I moan into her mouth as her expert touch sends waves of pleasure through me. My cock is going crazy at her touch, and I can't wait to be inside of her.

I pull my mouth from hers and kiss down her neck and across her collar bone. I massage her breasts, one in each hand, and I feel her nipples harden at my touch, grazing my palms and it's her turn to moan.

I let Ros jerk me off until I know that another minute of it and I won't be able to stop myself from coming. I pull her hand away from me and whisper into her hair.

"Your turn," I say.

I spin her around and pull her back against me, her back to my chest. I bring my hands around and play with her erect nipples, rolling them between my fingers and thumbs. I tease her this way for a while and then I move my hands lower. One of them stops on her belly and the other one keeps going down over her pubic bone and then I slip two fingers into her slit and rub over her already swollen clit. She sucks in a breath through her teeth as I make contact with her sensitive spot, and I smile at the sound.

I rub her clit, varying my movement from back to front to side to side and then into a circular motion. I vary the pressure I use, bringing Ros close to the edge and then pulling her back again.

I keep playing with her clit and I move my other hand lower until it passes my teasing hand. I reach lower and push three fingers into Ros. She's already dripping wet, and I can't help but moan when I feel how wet she is for me. Her wetness allows my fingers to fit inside of her easily and she whimpers my name as I begin to thrust my fingers in and out of her, hitting her g spot with each insertion. I move my fingers on her clit in time with the ones that are finger fucking her and this time, when she nears the edge, I don't pull her back.

I let her go over, screaming my name as she goes. I feel her clit pulsing beneath my fingers and her pussy tightens as a wave of warm wetness floods over my hand. Ros says my name, louder this time, and she grabs my forearms, her nails digging into the skin there and leaving little crescent moon shapes behind as she comes again.

I pull my fingers out of her pussy and away from her clit and she moans again, this time in disappointment and I grin.

"You really want this don't you?" I whisper into her ear where her head has fallen back onto my shoulder.

"Yes," she says.

"Tell me," I say. "Tell me how badly you want it."

"So badly," she says, her words broken by her panting for breath. "I need you to fill me up now. I want your cock inside of me."

"Your wish is my command," I say as a shiver of desire goes through me.

I walk toward the bed, taking Ros with me, but instead of getting onto it, I stop beside it and push Ros's shoulders forward and away from me. She quickly realizes what I want, and she happily obliges me, bending over and bracing herself on her palms, her ass and pussy on display for me.

I take a moment to look at her like that, spread and ready for me, moisture glistening on her lips and the tops of her thighs. I can't wait another moment and I take my cock in my hand and line the tip of it up with her opening. I push inside of her and instantly I'm consumed by her tightness. She feels so good around me; warm and wet and so fucking tight.

She makes a delicious ahh sound as I fill her up, and I pull almost all the way back out of her and then I slam back in, wanting to hear that noise again. Ros doesn't disappoint, and with each deep thrust that seems to take me further and further into her, she makes that delicious noise that sends shivers through my body.

I continue with long, slow strokes that tease us both, and when I can't stand the teasing any longer, I take hold of Ros's hips and begin to thrust faster, moving her hips with my hands in time with my thrusts. Ros pushes back against my thrusts too, pushing herself off her palms and taking my cock all the way inside of her.

I up my pace and slam into Ros hard and fast. Her noise has become almost a soundtrack to our fucking. Ahh. Ahh. Ahh. Hearing how turned on she is spurs me on even more and I hurtle toward my climax.

I'm fucking Ros so hard her elbows have given up on her and her body is on the bed, but still, she pushes herself back, meeting my desperate thrusts with an urgency of her own. She screams out my name and as she does, her pussy tightens around me, and I can't stop myself from coming any longer.

I stop, my cock all the way inside of Ros. I hold her hips in place as my cock pumps out my seed, filling Ros and emptying me. Pleasure shoots from my cock through my body and it's all I can do to stay upright as my orgasm takes me. I throw my head back, feeling the tendons standing out in my neck, and I growl Ros's name in an animalistic voice I almost don't even recognize as my own.

Ros's pussy is clenching and unclenching around me, drawing out my orgasm as her own hits her over again. I can see the duvet pulled into Ros's clenched fists and I can see her face where her head is turned to the side and half of it is resting on the bed. Her eyes are closed, her mouth twisted with ecstasy. As I watch, she gasps like a fish out of water, her mouth opening and closing, but her chest doesn't expand for a moment. When it does, she takes in a big breath and lets it out in a shuddering moan.

She clenches around me one last time and I feel a last blossoming of pleasure and then I slip out of her and we both clamber onto the bed. I lay on my side facing Ros. She's still on her front, her face turned toward me. At first, we don't speak, we just get our breath back.

"I've wanted to do that to you since I first set eyes on you," I say after a while.

"Bullshit," Ros says. "You hated me when we first met."

"I didn't exactly hate you. Just strong dislike," I say, and we both laugh. "But I'm serious about wanting to do that. Yes, you were annoying and a bit of a know it all, but I wanted to fuck you, and I figured it might actually keep you quiet for a minute."

Ros leans out and playfully punches my arm, but she laughs as she does it.

"I know what you mean," she says. "You were a total asshole in the beginning. You treated me like a slave, and you were always moaning about something I did or didn't do, but I still thought you were hot. I fantasized about killing you almost as much as I did fucking you, but here we are. I think I made the right choice in the end."

"I can't believe you plotted my murder. Talk about black widow shit," I say.

"Be careful. It's not too late to change my mind," Ros says with a fairly convincing evil laugh.

"I'm terrified," I say.

"No, you're not," Ros laughs. "You know you only have to shout, and you'll have Will in here saving you."

As she finishes her sentence, her face scrunches up and she slaps her forehead.

"Oh God. Will. He must have heard us," she says.

"Probably," I agree. "But don't worry. He's discreet."

"You sound like you know this from experience," Ros says.

I nod, and she frowns. I laugh, and her frown deepens.

"You can't be jealous about something that happened before we even met. Will has been my personal security for years," I say.

"I'm not jealous. Just mortified," Ros laughs.

"It could be worse," I point out. "It could be someone who doesn't know how to keep their mouth shut."

"True," I agree. "At least if Will is as discrete as you say he is, it won't be all around the office as soon as we're back."

"Ever," I correct her. "At least not from Will."

Ros considers this for a moment and then nods her head.

"Good," she says. "Because I'd hate the idea of being the topic of office gossip to stop us from doing that again." She pauses and then smiles at me. "And again. And again. And again. And… you get the idea."

"Are you saying you don't want this to be a moment of madness that we both go home and forget about?" I ask.

Ros nods her head.

"Yes," she says. "As much as I don't want to be gossiped about and I don't want people saying I'm getting any special treatment because I'm sleeping with the boss, I don't intend to let work run my whole life and not being with someone because of office gossip feels like I'm letting that happen. Does that make sense?"

It's my turn to nod. It does make sense and I know exactly what she means. She isn't the only one who let the office politics stop them from going after what they wanted once when Celia accused me of wanting to keep Ros on as my assistant because I liked her. I won't do it again either. Fuck Celia and anyone else who thinks they know better than I do how I feel and what I want.

"So, is that your way of asking me to date you?" I say with a smirk.

"It's my way of letting you know that I may be open to the

idea should you choose to ask me out," Ros says with an almost shy smile.

"Noted," I say. "I might even decide to take you up on it."

"Well don't wait too long, because the offer is time sensitive," Ros says.

I reach out and stroke her cheek and tuck a loose strand of hair behind her ear.

"Care for a date?" I ask.

"Yes," she says without hesitation and we both laugh. "Office consequences be damned."

"I like that line of thinking," I say. "But will you still feel this way when we're back in the office?"

"I think so," Ros says. She fidgets around for a moment and rolls onto her side facing me. "I know I'll still want to date you, but I might not be as chilled out about everyone at work knowing. So how about this. We'll date and go out and not worry about being seen by someone. But we won't actually tell anyone at the office or act differently around each other. At least not until we know it's serious."

"That works for me," I say.

I lean in and kiss Ros. She kisses me back and I start to put my arm around her, but she stops me and pulls her mouth from mine.

"I need to take my birth control," she says.

"Take it afterward," I say, not letting her go.

"And I still have work to do," she says.

"It'll still be there in the morning," I say, and I push her onto her back and get on top of her. I kiss her mouth and then her neck.

"I've been dating the boss for less than a minute and I'm already taking advantage," Ros says.

We laugh, and our laughter is cut short as I fit my mouth over Ros's and kiss her with a hunger that I don't feel will ever be sated, no matter how many times we do this. I keep kissing her, enjoying the feeling of her hands roaming over my back and sides. I kiss down her neck and chest and I scoot backward on the bed, planting kisses on her body all the way down her stomach.

I stop between her legs and push them wider open until her slit is spread wide open. She is already wet, and I moan with longing as I smell her desire as I move my face toward her. I lick from her pussy to her clit and it's her turn to moan. I work her clit with my tongue, relishing the taste of her juices as I make her come undone beneath me.

CHAPTER
Fourteen

ROS

Alex and I have been secretly dating now for a couple of weeks and everything is going great. Having Will trailing us on our dates was weird at first, but I've kind of gotten used to him being there and fading into the background now, and true to Alex's words, Will is really discreet. Our secret is still very much a secret at work, and I like that, although I feel secure enough in what Alex and I have at this point that if it got out at work, I would just live with the teasing rather than end the relationship.

Today is Saturday and Alex is taking me out for the day. He says it's a surprise and he won't tell me where we're going or what we're going to be doing. The only clue I got was to wear something casual that I was comfortable in and wasn't going to hinder me moving around. God, he made it sound like we were going to be doing an assault course or something. I really hope that's not it.

I took his advice, and I'm wearing blue jeggings with a yellow tank top and white sneakers. I have my cell phone and keys in one pocket and cash and a credit card in the other one, so I don't need to carry a purse. I can move about easily and

I'm comfortable. Well physically I'm comfortable. Mentally I'm now worried Alex thinks my idea of a good time is an assault course. No, I think to myself, shaking my head. Even the worst-case scenario isn't that bad. There's no way he would take me to do something like that because he knows I would hate it. Plus, for something like that, surely, he would have warned me to bring exercise clothes.

I'm waiting outside of my building for him because it's a beautiful day, the sun is shining, and I want to enjoy the fresh air while I wait. Alex is never late so it's not like I'll have to stand out here for long anyway. Sure enough, right on the dot of ten thirty am, Alex pulls up in front of my building.

I go over to the car and get in. He leans over and kisses me hello, and then he pulls away and heads away from my building.

"Come on then, spill," I say. "Where are we going?"

"You'll see," Alex replies with a smile.

I make a face at him, and he laughs.

"Be patient," he says.

"I would be, but it's not really in my nature," I tell him.

"No shit," he says, and I stick my tongue out at him.

"Stop that or I'll make good use of it," Alex says and my clit tingles deliciously even as I grin and put my tongue back away in my mouth.

We drive for about twenty minutes and then Alex pulls onto the coastal road.

"The beach?" I ask.

I don't expect Alex to either confirm or deny this, and I'm not wrong. He just glances at me and grins and then he looks back at the road. I watch out of the window for any clues as to what we might be doing besides going to the beach but there's nothing that jumps out at me as an obvious choice.

Finally, Alex pulls into a large parking lot in front of the entrance to a theme park. Over it is a large archway with the name, "Bertie's Beachside Bonanza" displayed in a red, cartoonish font beside a smiling clown that gives me the creeps.

"Well? What do you think?" Alex asks. "I know it looks a bit rough from here, but it's actually a really cool place."

I can't help but smile at his excited expression. I haven't been to a theme park in years, but I'm not against the idea, and I nod.

"Good choice," I say.

"Thank God for that," Alex says. "There's an outdoor theater doing Hamlet around the corner and if you had looked repulsed at the idea of the theme park, I was going to take you there and pretend that had been my plan all along, but I can't say it's something I'd have enjoyed."

"Sneaky," I laugh. "Nothing like hedging your bets."

"It's always best to be one step ahead of the game," Alex says. "Now come on. Let's go and be kids again. You have no idea how hard it was for me to convince Will I'd be fine for one day without security and I intend to make the most of it."

"Is that really a good idea?" I ask.

"Sure," Alex says. "Like I said to Will, who would be looking for someone with money at a place like this?"

"Fair point," I admit with a laugh.

We get out of the car and instantly I smell that heady theme park mix of frying meat and onions, cotton candy and mini donuts, all mixed with the salty tang of the sea. It takes me back to my childhood with one deep breath. The air is ringing with the whoosh of rides, the thump thump thump of the bass coming from the rides and the screams of joy and terror from the riders.

We reach the arch and there's a small blue ticket booth with a bored looking attendant sitting there, taking money and issuing tickets. A small line has formed, and we join it. It moves quickly and Alex asks for two tickets and within minutes we have them, and we're inside the park.

"What do you want to do first?" Alex asks me.

I look around and smile and point at the highest track of the biggest roller coaster.

"I want to ride that," I say.

"Nothing like starting out big," Alex laughs.

He takes my hand, and we walk over to the roller coaster. The line here is a lot longer than the one to get into the park and I'm glad for the warm day. A group of teenagers stand in front of us in the line laughing and egging each other on to be the first one to back out of riding the immense roller coaster. None of them drop out of the line, although judging by the pale faces on a couple of them, I think they might like to if there was a way to do it without losing face in front of their friends.

Almost forty minutes passes and then finally, it's our turn. I feel my stomach turn with a mixture of excitement and nerves as Alex and I reach the roller coaster's car. He gestures for me to get seated first and I do, and then he plops down beside me. Laughter and little screams come from all around us, and the attendant walks the length of the car and checks all the safety harnesses are in the correct position. When he's satisfied, he gives a thumbs up to the other man in the control booth who returns the gesture. The roller coaster car beneath us seems to vibrate slightly and then there's a sound like the releasing of steam and we start to move.

We climb the huge tracks and I swallow hard as the people below us become the size of tiny little peanuts littering the ground. The cars and nearby buildings look like toy ones, and by the time we reach the top, I'm starting to regret my choice of ride.

We reach the top and the car pauses there for a moment and then the drop begins. I raise my hands in the air with everyone else, screaming in delight as my stomach rolls and we plunge down toward the ground. My regret has completely gone, and I laugh as I feel the wind in my face. I always feel so wild and free on roller coasters, and it's been too long since I last rode one.

The tracks take us through a series of loops and dips and turns and a few more drops, though none as big as that first mega drop. By the time the ride ends, I already want to go on it again. I forgot how much of an adrenaline junkie I was as a teenager when we would come to these types of places on the school vacations.

I get off the roller coaster with slightly shaky legs, laughing and running my fingers through my hair, trying to get it back into some sort of order.

"That was awesome," I say.

"Agreed," Alex says. "We need to ride that again at least one more time before we leave."

"Good plan," I say. "Now it's your turn to choose what we ride next."

Alex looks around a bit and then he grins.

"Ready to get wet?" he says.

"Always," I purr.

"Not like that you dirty minded thing," Alex laughs. He nods toward the log flume. "Like that."

"Sure, why not," I say. "The sun is warm enough to dry us pretty quickly."

CHAPTER
Fifteen

ROS

We head for the ride hand in hand laughing like children. The line for this ride is much shorter than the one for the roller coaster and within about ten minutes, we're seated and floating around the ride. As we move, small water pistols fire streams of water at us from the sides of the ride and at one point, we move beneath what looks like a giant shower head that sprinkles water on us. All in all though, except for a few splashes, we are mostly still dry when we come to the drop.

The ride plunges downward, heading for the plunge pool at the bottom. It hits it and water shoots up on either side of us. I'm sitting behind Alex, and I wrap my arms around him and bury my face in his back and I come away reasonably unscathed. When we step off the ride, I see how wet Alex is and I can't help but laugh as he flicks away the drops of water from his hair.

"You cheated," he laughs.

"No, I used the resources available to me," I correct him.

He flicks some of the water at me and I shriek and dodge it. We walk through a section of the park that is dedicated to children's rides. It's nice to hear their excited laughter on the rides and it's nice to have a moment of relative quiet with Alex as we chat. We reach the end of the kid's part and pass a food truck. The smell is delicious and my stomach growls. Alex looks down at it and laughs.

"I guess that means you're hungry," he says.

"I blame all of these delicious smells," I say. "Besides, it's law that you can't come to a theme park without getting a cheeseburger."

"Is that so?" Alex says and I nod solemnly. "Well, I have always considered myself to be a law-abiding citizen so two cheeseburgers it is. Do you want to grab us a table?"

I look around and spot an empty picnic table. I make my way over to it and sit down. I don't have long to wait before Alex appears with two cheeseburgers and two sodas. I'm glad to see that he thought to buy drinks too as I am pretty thirsty.

I thank Alex and take my drink and my cheeseburger. I have a long drink and then I unwrap my burger. I take a bite and moan. It's so delicious.

"Oh my God, that's so good," I say after I chew and swallow my bite.

Alex nods his head as he chews and then swallows.

"Why is it that theme park burgers taste better than literally any other burger?" he says.

"I don't know," I say. "But you are totally right that they do."

We make short work of the juicy burgers and drink down our sodas.

"Something gentle now until that settles a bit?" I ask.

Alex nods his head.

"I know just the thing," he says. "Come on."

He gets up and holds his hand out to me. I take it and he pulls me to my feet, and we set off. Alex leads me to where he wants me to go, and I smile when I realize where that is. The bumper cars.

We get into a car each when it's our turn and we spend the next five minutes or so driving around the little stage and bumping into each other and jamming each other against the sides. For the whole time, all I do is laugh and smile and when the ride finishes, I'm still laughing as I get out of the car and make my way off the driving area.

We spend the next few hours going on more roller coasters, including another ride on the giant roller coaster we rode first. When we're sick of the roller coasters, we take a turn on the tilt-a-whirl, and I come off so dizzy that I have to cling to Alex to stop me from falling over. Alex leads me to a wooden bench and deposits me there, telling me he'll be back in a second. I assume he's going to use the bathroom or something, but when he comes back, he has two huge green and yellow portions of cotton candy on sticks. He hands one to me and I thank him.

I take a bite and let the sugar melt on my tongue. After a moment, I put my tongue out at Alex.

"What color is it?" I say, putting it back in my mouth.

"Green," he laughs. "What about mine?"

He sticks his tongue out for a second and I laugh.

"The same," I tell him.

"My grandad always brought me here when I was little," Alex says after a moment of silence. "I always got cotton candy and it had to be the green and yellow one, because I was awkward, and the pink and blue colored one was everywhere so I had to be different."

"I can't imagine your grandfather riding roller coasters," I say with a smile.

"Oh God no, he never would," Alex says. "We used to bring my cousins too, so that I had someone to go on the rides with. It was always one of my favorite places."

"You should call your cousins and arrange to bring your grandad back here for a day out," I say. "As a surprise."

"Yeah, he'd love that," Alex grins. "And I might get to meet his new girlfriend."

"Girlfriend?" I ask.

"That's why he took early retirement. Well, early for him. He met someone," Alex says. "It's going really well. They're on some sort of cruise at the minute."

"Aww good for him," I say, and I mean it. Mr. Waters deserves to be happy.

"Yeah, I love that he's found someone to enjoy his retirement with," Alex says.

"Shame there's no tunnel of love here. Maybe we could have persuaded them to ride it," I say with a grin.

"I doubt you'd have persuaded him," Alex says, also laughing.

"Worth a shot though. I can be persuasive when I want to be," I say.

Alex is still laughing, and he rolls his eyes.

"Yeah, he'd probably do it for you as well," he says, but it's good natured and there's no trace of jealousy or bitterness in his tone. "Right. Let's get moving. There's still so much we haven't done yet. Where to next?"

I think for a moment and then I take Alex's hand and lead him back into the crowds in the park. I spotted the top of this one as we got onto the tilt-a-whirl and made a mental note to choose it the next time it was my turn to choose. I lead Alex right up to it and he groans.

"The ghost train? Seriously?" he says.

I nod.

"Yup," I say. "What's wrong? Are you scared?"

"Terrified," Alex says and shakes his head. "Nah it's just lame."

"It is so not lame. It's fun," I say. "Come on, don't be

boring." I lean in closer and whisper in Alex's ear. "Who knows where my hands could wander to in the dark."

Alex looks at me and raises an eyebrow and I just smile.

"Come on then," he says, taking me to join the line.

Again, it's a shorter line than the ones the roller coasters have, and we get on the ride reasonably quickly. After the attendant has checked our restraints and the engine fires up, I nudge Alex with my elbow.

"See, I told you I could be pretty persuasive when I wanted to be," I say.

"I hope that's not what you would have said to persuade my grandad," Alex says with a snort of laughter, and I shake my head and playfully slap his arm, but I can't help but laugh along with him and we're still laughing as the ride starts and we go through a plastic sheet and are plunged into darkness.

At first, nothing much happens, then a spotlight flashes on, showing a model of a witch that jumps forward and screams in our faces. I scream back and Alex and I both laugh. As we move deeper into the haunted house, more spotlights flash on, and more things jump out and scare us. Things hanging from the roof above us tickle our skin and small jets of water are fired at us.

We come to another of those plastic sheets and the car pushes through it and we're outside again. I blink at the sudden brightness and then we're heading down, and I scream again as my stomach rolls. I've barely gotten over my shock at the drop when we go back inside of the place and back into the darkness.

A skeleton jumps out at us, its bones lighting up a sickly neon green in the darkness. Another spotlight comes on and a giant tarantula waves its front legs at us. As it does, a smaller spider plops down into Alex's lap and he screams and goes to flick it away, only for it to get pulled back up into the roof. I can't help but laugh at Alex's scream and he laughs too after he gets over the shock.

"I really thought that was real," he says through the laughter.

We emerge back into the brightness of the day still laughing and go down one more drop and then the ride ends, and we exit the car and walk away. I'm still laughing as we dodge our way through the crowd.

"See it wasn't that lame, was it?" I ask. "It sure scared you."

"It didn't scare me, I just got a jump is all," Alex insists. "And I also noticed the lack of your hands coming over to my side of the car like you hinted they might."

"I hinted at no such thing," I say, pretending to be shocked at his suggestion. "I merely said that my hands might wander in the dark. I didn't say where to."

"You implied it," Alex says.

"Maybe, but that's not a promise is it? Besides, I wouldn't have dared to touch you in there in case I scared you," I laugh, and Alex makes a face at me.

"I was going to say we should play some games, see if we can win you a cuddly toy, but I don't know if you deserve one now," Alex says.

"Hmm, I think I do," I say.

"Why?" Alex asks.

I shrug one shoulder.

"I don't know. I just want one," I admit, and we laugh again.

"Come on then," Alex says, and we head toward the nearest game booths.

We spend over an hour moving between the games, shooting guns and water pistols, throwing darts and hoops, hooking ducks and knocking coconuts off posts. By the end of it, I have a yellow duckling stuffed toy and a keyring with a photo of me and Alex in it. By the time we've finished playing, it's starting to get dark, and the sea breeze is bringing a chill to the air.

"Do you want to grab some food and then get out of here?" Alex says.

I nod and we head over to the food court, this time looking for somewhere to sit inside and eat. We choose a bar and grill place and I order a lemon and herb chicken breast with fries and Alex orders a rib eye with baked potato. The food comes out quickly and it's delicious. I am so hungry, and I put it down to the sea air and the excitement. It seems like Alex feels the same way, because we both attack our meals and barely speak a word as we eat except to comment on how good the food is.

"Oh, Alex look," I say when we've almost finished eating.

I point to a poster on the wall beside our booth. Tonight, at nine thirty, there's a firework display in the theme park. I look at my watch.

"It's just after eight. What do you stay?" I ask.

"I don't mind staying as long as you're not cold," he says. "I don't even have a jacket to give you."

"I'm ok," I say. "I did feel a bit chilly there, but I'm ok now. I think maybe it was just because I needed to eat something hot."

"Ok. Are you ready to go back out there then?" Alex asks and I nod.

He signals to our waitress, and she brings the bill which he pays. I've learned my lesson with trying to pay for things when I'm out on a date with Alex. Ok, that sounds bad, doesn't it? It's not like he hurt me or anything, he just made it clear that he wants to spoil me, not the other way around, and that he can afford to do it. I did argue the point, but in the end, it was easier just to give in, and I've found different ways to return the favor that don't involve money like the hour-long massage I gave Alex the other night, or the fact that I washed his car for him. He seems to like those kinds of gestures and I like that I can do something nice for him like he does for me.

We leave the bar and grill and start walking. Although I wasn't lying to Alex back there about being warm, I am soon feeling the chill again. I don't say anything because I don't want to ruin our fun, but Alex must see the goosebumps on my arms because he takes my hand and changes direction abruptly.

"You're cold," he says. "Come on. I know where we can keep warm until the fireworks start without just sitting in a bar or something boring."

I allow him to lead me to wherever he has in mind and when we get to the entrance to the hall of mirrors, I can't help but giggle.

"Really?" I ask. "I didn't think you'd like anything like this."

"I don't mind it," Alex says. "And it's out of the cold."

We enter and step into the first hallway. It's empty except for us, giving us plenty of time to look in each of the mirrors. We point and laugh as we turn tall and skinny to the point of almost disappearing, and then short and dumpy and then normal but with a huge head and then with a tiny pin head. Some of them are really good and convincing and by the end of the first hallway, my cheeks are aching from laughing so much. Alex is laughing too, and I'm pleased that he's having a good time in here and isn't just doing it to humor me so that I don't get cold.

We move into the next hallway and again, we are the only people in the hallway although I can hear voices and laughter both up ahead and behind us. They must time it so each little group or couple gets their own time in each part of the place. We are halfway along when Alex looks to his left and then his right. He establishes we are alone, and I think he's going to kiss me or something, but instead, he reaches out and puts his fingers into a little groove in the side of one of the mirrors that I hadn't even noticed. He pulls and the mirror opens like a door.

"I love that this still works," he says. "We used to go back here when we were kids."

"Are we allowed to do that?" I ask.

"Nope," he says and then he takes my hand and steps through the door.

"What are you doing?" I hiss as I'm pulled along behind Alex.

"This," he says, closing the door and then fitting his lips over mine.

He kisses me deeply, leaving me breathless when he pulls away.

"Have you noticed something?" he says.

"What?" I ask.

"It's dark in here too," he says.

"So it is," I say, and I reach out and rub his cock through his jeans.

I can feel it hardening even through the thick denim and I grin to myself and open his button and fly and push my hand inside of his boxers. I feel so daring and adventurous doing this here, where we aren't even supposed to be and the feeling, mixed with the desire I feel for Alex makes me quickly lose my inhibitions.

Alex kisses me again as I move my fist up and down his cock. I enjoy the feel of him getting even harder as I work him and when he pulls his mouth from mine, I love the sound of him gasping as I bring him close to climax. I keep his cock in my hand, still working him and I move closer to him so that I can whisper in his ear.

"Fuck me, Alex," I say.

"Here?" he says, sounding surprised.

"Here," I confirm.

Even as I say it, I'm wiggling my jeggings and panties down. I kick off one sneaker and pull that leg clear of my clothes. It's all we need for easy access and it's all I plan on doing. I might be feeling adventurous, but I am not stripping off in a place where it's dark enough that I might not be able to find my clothes again.

Alex cups my ass in his hands and then he lifts me in the air, and I wrap my arms around his shoulders and my legs around his waist. He pushes inside of me and presses me up against the back of the mirrored door. He begins to pump into me, and I cling to him, thrusting my hips with his, needing to feel him filling me all the way up. Alex pumps faster and I know he's almost there, because I had brought him to the edge with my hand before he even got inside of me. His breathing is ragged, and he whispers my name and moans.

He pushes a hand between us and as he pumps, he massages my clit and I'm soon caught up to where he is and when we climax, it's a rush for both of us together. We cling to each other as pleasure fills us. I press my face into Alex's neck and murmur his name as my body tingles with pleasure and my clit sends sparks throughout the rest of my body. My orgasm is over all too soon, and Alex puts me down and I put my leg back into my panties and jeggings.

"Holy shit that was amazing," Alex says as he zips his jeans up.

"Was it worth waiting for?" I ask.

"God yeah. It was way better than a grope on the ghost train," he says.

I push my foot into my sneaker and tell Alex I'm ready. He pushes the door open and peeks out and looks both ways.

"All clear," he says.

He steps out and I follow him, and right as I step into the

hallway, another couple appears at the end of it. Alex and I look at each other as the couple watch us in surprise. We both burst into laughter and Alex quickly closes the door and I link my arm through his and we scurry off to the next hallway, laughing and leaning into each other.

I look down at my clothes and see I'm pretty much dressed properly as is Alex, but I dread to think how much my hair gave us away to that couple back there. I reach up with my free hand and tidy it up a bit and we make our way through the rest of the hallways. We pop out and an attendant smiles at us as we leave.

"Did you enjoy it?" he asks.

"Yes, thank you," I say.

"Easily the best thing we have done all day," Alex says.

I punch him playfully in the arm and we both laugh again, and the attendant looks bemused by us, but he shrugs and lets us go on our way. We are clearly satisfied customers so he's happy. He probably thinks we're drunk or something. Hopefully he doesn't guess the truth. And hopefully there are no cameras back there. No there won't be. If there was going to be, they would be in the attraction itself and we would have been seen sneaking off behind the scenes and we would have been stopped before we even had time to get properly started.

"What time is it?" I ask as we head toward the central arena where the fireworks will be. We aren't the only ones heading in that direction and I figure it must be close to the time they are due to start.

"It's just after ten past nine," Alex says. "Do you want to try and fit one more ride in, or just go to the arena?"

"Let's just go to the arena," I say. "Loads of people are heading that way and we want seats."

Alex nods his head, and we keep walking. We reach the arena and go inside. It's designed like an old Roman arena with a large central circle for whatever show is taking place, surrounded on all sides by seating. Every few feet there are steps leading up to the higher tiers. The seats are concrete benches, but they look clean and comfortable enough, and up in the canopy above, halogen lights burn, sending down a lovely warmth.

Alex and I choose seats about halfway up the seating so we have a good view and aren't too high up where the fireworks might be spoiled slightly by the lights. I snuggle against his side, and he wraps his arm around my shoulders.

Right on time, a loud blast of music bursts out and I know by the laughter around me that I'm not the only one who jumped at the loud sound.

"Ladies and gentlemen, boys and girls, get ready for the display," a voice booms out and then the music starts up again.

There's a hissing noise then a fizzing sound followed by a bang and then the first firework has gone off. Soon we're surrounded by whizzing and banging, plus the sound of the crowd oohing and aahing at the sights. The fireworks are amazing, all colors of the rainbow and golds and silvers and purples and the sparks dance together, making patterns in the sky.

Alex and I sit with our arms around each other watching the show and when it's finally over, I'm a little bit sad that we have to release each other. Alex leans down and kisses my forehead and then he leads me down the nearest steps and out of the arena. We head back toward the parking lot as part of a fairly large crowd, although a lot of people still linger around the rides and game booths.

"Thank you," I say.

"For what?" Alex asks.

"This," I say. "It's been the perfect day."

"And it's not over yet," Alex says. "Do you really think

that quickie in the hall of mirrors is it for the night? Oh no my love, that was just a warmup. Get ready for us to make our own fireworks when we get back to my place."

I can't help but start to walk quicker and Alex laughs and keeps pace with me. My pussy is already wet, and I want him so badly. Making our own fireworks between the sheets will be the perfect end to the most amazing day.

CHAPTER
Sixteen

ALEX

I wake up and stretch. I wince as my muscles are pulled out and I cut my stretch short. Two days have gone by since Ros and I went to the theme park, and I'm still aching all over from it. I smile to myself. It was worth every second of the pain. Not only was the day itself a lot of fun (and I don't just mean the quickie we had behind the scenes in the hall of mirrors either although I'm not saying that wasn't fun), but the sex we had that night was mind blowing, and it continued on into yesterday where we spent most of the day in bed at my place. We only moved to use the bathroom and get food all day until about five o'clock when Ros announced she needed to come home and get fresh clothes and stuff for work today. Instead of her leaving here and collecting her stuff and then coming back, we decided I'd bring my stuff here to her place and after we shared a long, hot shower, we resumed staying in bed together, although it was a different bed.

I'd love to have another day like that one today, but it's Monday and duty calls. Still though, we have another half an hour or so before the alarm goes off and we have to get up and start getting ready. Half an hour isn't long enough, but it's better than nothing and I can definitely think of better things to do to fill it than laying here staring up at the ceiling.

I turn toward Ros who is sleeping on her side facing away from me. I gently pull the duvet down a bit and expose her shoulders and her upper back. I move in closer and put my arm around her. I nuzzle her neck and kiss along her shoulder. She moans and shuffles a bit and I run my tongue back along her shoulder and up her neck. I nibble on her ear lobe.

"Good morning," she mumbles, her voice still thick with sleep.

"Not yet it isn't. But it's going to be," I say with a grin and then I resume kissing Ros's neck.

She moans and stretches out and then she pushes herself back against me. My already hard cock presses against her ass cheeks and I feel myself getting even harder as she wiggles her ass, rubbing it over me. I run my hand down the front of her body and push it between her legs. I push my fingers into her slit and begin to massage her clit.

She lifts her top leg slightly, making it easier for me to get access to her clit, and I'm quite happy to oblige her, and I keep rubbing her from side to side. She moans and writhes as I bring her toward her orgasm. I can tell she's almost there by the way her breathing changes and the way her clit seems to pulse beneath my fingers. She surprises me though. Instead of laying back against me and letting her orgasm wash over her, she shifts away from me slightly, making room for her to roll toward me.

She moves my hand out of the way and then she pushes herself up onto her knees, pushes me onto my back by my shoulders, and straddles me. She is a sight to behold. She's fucking glorious in fact. Her flawless skin is flushed pink, partly I think from the heat of the night and partly from desire. Her makeup free face is still slightly puffy from her pillow, but she's gorgeous, her skin dewy and radiant and her whole look just makes me want to grab her and fuck her forever.

She smiles as she bends at the waist and runs her lips against mine. Her touch is so feather light, I'm not certain if she is actually touching me or not. I lift my head up off the pillow slightly and go to kiss her harder, but she moves back as I come toward her and shakes her head.

"You just lay there and enjoy yourself," she says.

I think she knows that me laying here, experiencing her touch and not being able to touch her back, is going to be absolute torture as well as enjoyable. Oh well. I can think of much worse ways in which I could be tortured. Bring it on.

Ros leans back down, and I feel her feather light touch against my lips once more. I ache to grab her and kiss her hard, to throw her on the ground and fuck her brains out, but I force myself to resist the urge and just enjoy the slow torture I'm being given.

Ros moves her lips down my neck and then over my chest. She pauses at my chest to flick her tongue over both of my nipples in turn until they both stand at attention and the tingly feeling from them wakes up other nerve endings in my body, making me crave her touch somewhere much more intimate.

Done with my nipples, she scoots backward so she's straddling my knees rather than my cock and she kisses a trail down my belly toward my cock. I hold my breath in anticipation as she reaches the very bottom of my belly, but instead of kissing along my cock, she skips it altogether and kisses the inside of my thigh. She scoots backward again and licks and nibbles her way down my inside thigh to my knee.

Her touch is both torture and delight. She's waking up my full body, making me ready to feel my pleasure on a whole new level and I'm helpless to stop her. Not that I want to stop her. Except maybe to fuck her brains out sooner than she had planned on it.

She moves her mouth to my other leg and works her way back up that inner thigh until her face hovers over my cock and unless she's going to start on my calves or my arms, my cock is all that's left for her to plant her little kisses on. She doesn't disappoint. She starts at the base of my cock and kisses her way to the tip, where she runs her tongue around it in a circular motion before licking her way back down the length. She kisses back up me and puts her lips on the tip of me. She's just starting to take my length into the warmth of her mouth when the alarm goes off and she jumps away from me, startled by the sound.

"Fuck," I say. I reach out and switch the alarm off. "You have got to be fucking kidding me."

"To be continued," Ros says. "What I have in mind for you is going to take longer than the few minutes we have until the snooze alarm goes off."

I start to tell her that she can't leave me like this, aching for her and frustrated, but she seems to feel the same way because she's moving back up me and she's straddling my cock once more.

"We'll just have to finish quickly for now," she says with a wink.

"I mean I'm disappointed, but at the same time, I'm not," I say and Ros smiles.

"You don't need to be disappointed. You have instant gratification and something to look forward to," she says, and she winks at me, and then she lifts herself up, takes my cock in her fist and lines it up with her pussy, and then she lowers herself onto me, impaling herself on my cock, and any words I was planning on saying to her are gone from my mind. The only think I'm thinking of right now is how utterly fucking amazing Ros's warm, tight pussy feels wrapped around my cock.

I know I'm not going to last as long as I would like to. Ros's teasing touch already has me on the edge and the feel of her wetness wrapped around me only pushes me closer. As she begins to move up and down on my cock, the view of her is so amazing, it takes my breath away. Her breasts bounce in time with her thrusts and her taut stomach is pulled so flat that I can see the muscles beneath the skin. Her face and neck are flushed, and she looks down at me and smirks and then she ups the pace of her movement on me.

She pushes her fingers between her lips and plays with her clit as she moves on me and the sight of her pleasuring herself while pleasuring me at the same time is almost more than I can take. She isn't wasting any time here and she brings herself to the edge quickly. I feel her go over the edge as she tightens around me, and I moan out her name as I grab her hips and hold her in place on my cock as I orgasm too.

I keep my eyes open as I come, watching as Ros comes too. Her eyes are closed, and her head is tilted back slightly. Her mouth is open and she's gasping, moaning as she breathes out. A shudder goes through her and her breasts dance deliciously and then she opens her eyes and smiles down at me.

"Now is it a good morning?" she says.

"Oh yes," I reply.

She leans forward and kisses me. She pulls back and the snooze alarm goes off.

"Better timing than the first one," she says with a laugh and then she's up and off me, her warmth replaced with cool air. "I'm going for a shower. I won't be long."

She flounces out of the bedroom, and I watch her tight little ass as she goes. When she's out of sight, I sit up and run my hands over my face. That was definitely a good way to start the day, but it's made me want to skip work and just stay here with Ros even more. I know she'll never agree to it though – she'll say she's taking advantage of being with the boss and she won't see that it isn't necessarily a bad thing.

I know I won't be able to persuade her, and I decide I won't even try to because then we'll only end up having an argument and that's the last thing I want to do. I get up and grab last night's boxer shorts off the chair where I put them last night with the rest of my clothes when I got ready for bed. I throw them on just so I'm not naked on the walk to the bathroom for my shower when Ros is done. Normally I wouldn't bother, but I know she has a roommate, and I heard her moving around in her room when I woke up for a pee in the night, so I know she's here.

I sit back down on the bed with my back against the headboard and my legs stretched out in front of me. I don't get underneath the duvet – it's warm enough to just enjoy the air on me. I hear the water switch off in the bathroom and not long later, the bedroom door opens, and Ros comes back in.

Her body is wrapped in a towel that starts above her breasts and finishes at her mid-thigh, and her hair is wrapped in another towel. Her skin is pink from the heat of the shower, and she smells faintly of strawberries as she passes me. She looks and smells good enough to eat and I reach out to grab her, but she swiftly jumps to one side.

"You know we don't have time for that," Ros says.

I shrug my shoulders.

"So, let's be late. It's not like anyone can tell us off," I say.

"You know why I can't," Ros says.

I remember my earlier thought about not getting into an argument about this and I decide to give in, but not before making her laugh first.

"Ok, how about this. We stay here and fuck all morning and then I give you a written warning for being late," I say.

Ros snorts laughter and shakes her head.

"With an offer like that, how can I refuse?" she says.

"I mean I don't know," I say. "But I still have a feeling that you're going to."

"Got it in one," she says.

"You can't blame me for trying," I say.

I hop up off the bed and go up behind Ros where she sits at her dressing table applying cream to her face. I kiss her exposed shoulder.

"I won't be long," I say. "Don't miss me too much."

"I'll try not to," she says, smiling at my reflection in the mirror.

I leave her to it, leaving the bedroom and closing the door behind me. I'm almost in the bathroom when another door opens and a short, curvy girl with bright green eyes appears in front of me.

"I take it you're Alex?" she says.

I nod.

"Yeah," I say. "I like that you knew that. It means I'm the only half-naked man you expect to catch coming from Ros's bedroom."

She smiles but then she gets serious again.

"Ros is my best friend," she says. "And she's been through a lot with men."

"Ok," I say, not sure what else to say, but conscious of the fact she is blocking my path to the bathroom, and I'm dressed only in my boxer shorts. Thank God I chose to put them on. This could have been a whole hell of a lot more awkward if I hadn't.

"I'm just warning you. Don't hurt my friend or I will make you wish you had never even met her. And don't let the fact that you're like twice as tall as I am make you think I can't do it," she says.

She doesn't wait for an answer. She sidesteps around me

and heads toward the living room of the apartment. I look back over my shoulder at her.

"It was a pleasure to meet you Fiona," I say.

She gives me the finger over her shoulder without even turning around and I grin. I'm still grinning as I go into the bathroom. I feel as though I should be annoyed at Fiona's little spiel, but the truth is, I can't help but think it's kind of sweet, and I like that Ros has such a good friend who is looking out for her. I have no intention of hurting her, but that doesn't mean it isn't good to have someone who has her back as well as I do.

As I shower, I debate telling Ros how good of a friend Fiona is to her, but I decide against it because Ros will likely not think it's sweet and she will probably get pissed off at Fiona for overstepping the mark like that and I don't want the women to fight over this.

I finish my shower and use the toilet and then brush my teeth. I go back to the bedroom and see Ros has gone. I dress quickly and go to find her. She's sitting at the table with Fiona. They're both eating cereal and sipping coffee, and a third bowl and spoon sit beside a steaming cup of coffee. I sit down in front of it.

"Thanks," I say, pouring some cereal into the bowl.

"Fiona, this is Alex. Alex, this is Fiona," Ros says.

"We already met," Fiona says, surprising me. "I've warned him if he hurts you, he will have me to deal with."

"Oh God Fi, no," Ros says, but she too surprises me, because instead of getting angry, she bursts into laughter as she turns to me. "Sorry about her, Alex. But the fact you're still here tells me you've realized she's more chihuahua than rottweiler."

"Are you kidding me? Rottweilers are big babies. Chihuahuas are the spawn of the devil," I say.

"Only if someone hurts their friend," Fiona puts in and the three of us laugh.

Ok, so Fiona isn't going to be the cold enemy I thought she was going to be, but I still don't doubt that she will find a way to carry out her threat if I hurt Ros. Which I have no intention of.

We finish our breakfast and Ros and I get ready to leave. When we're ready, Ros opens the front door and Will greets her. She jumps and he apologizes, and she turns to me.

"Have you seriously left him out here all night?" she says.

She's getting used to Will's presence and she's even getting used to the fact that he is meant to blend into the background, not be a part of our social group, but it seems like this one is still a step too far for her.

"At the very least he could have slept on the couch," she says.

"Relax," Will says. "I've only been here five minutes. I've just started my shift."

"Ok," Ros says. "But if you ever do end up doing an overnight shift here, please let me know so you can come inside."

Will nods his head but I already know he won't do it. Just like he hasn't lied to Ros – he really has just started his shift – but he failed to mention the fact that he took over from one of his team who had the night shift and did indeed stand in this hallway all night.

CHAPTER
Seventeen

ALEX

I sit at my desk and debate whether or not it's a good idea. I grin to myself and decide that fuck it, it's definitely a good idea. It's not like anyone but Ros will see it and if she chooses not to do it, as I assume she will, I still think it will make her laugh. And if she chooses to do it, well that's a definite bonus.

I add "give your boss a blow job" to Ros's lists of tasks that I need her to complete today, like I wanted to do when we first met, and I go and put it on her desk. I have purposely waited until I know she'll be having her morning coffee break before I leave the note on her desk, because I don't want to be there when she sees that entry. I want her to see it and get a kick out of it without having to look at me while she does it.

I go back to my office and get on with what I have to do. I type out a few emails and then I return a call.

"Mikaelson's Music, Greta speaking, how can I help you?" a woman says, answering my call.

"Hi Greta," I say. "It's Alex Waters from Waters' Financial here. I'm returning Mr. Mikaelson's call."

"Let me see if he's available," Greta says. "Is it ok to put you on hold for a moment?"

"Sure," I say.

I sit and wait while Greta no doubt goes straight to Mr. Mikaelson, knowing he is there, and asking him if he wants to take this call or not. I can't be annoyed by it – it's the way the world works, and Ros does the same for me. Plus, it's not like I need Mr. Mikaelson for something. He's the one who wants to speak to me so it's his call really.

My office door opens while I'm waiting, and Ros comes in. She smiles and comes toward my desk, but she doesn't say anything, and she doesn't seem to have anything for me to look at or sign or anything.

"Are you ok?" I ask her as she approaches my desk.

She nods her head, still smiling at me and still not speaking. She reaches my desk and instead of sitting down, she comes around to my side of it. She leans down and runs her tongue along my neck. Goosebumps rush to the surface of my skin and my cock reacts to her touch, hardening as she sucks on my skin gently.

"Ros, what the hell?" I ask.

"I'm just finishing up my to-do list," she says with a smirk that sends a shiver of desire through me.

She takes hold of the back of my chair and spins it around so that I'm facing her with my back to my desk. She kneels on the ground between my feet and pushes my knees apart.

"Ros, anyone could come to my door," I say.

She shrugs.

"Don't tell them to come in then," she replies.

I'm surprised at how chilled out she is about the idea of being disturbed but I don't have long to dwell on it because she's already unbuttoned my pants.

"I'm on the phone," I say as she gets the pants open and tugs at them.

"Lift your ass up," she says.

"After I'm done on the phone," I say.

"Now or never," she says.

She tugs hard on my pants, and I'm actually scared they are going to rip so I lift my ass up and quick as a flash, my pants and boxer shorts are down to my ankles. Ros grabs my cock in her fist and lowers her head, her tongue flicking over the tip. I moan as pleasure radiates out from her touch and I close my eyes as she sucks my tip into her mouth and then bobs her head down, taking my length into her mouth too. She doesn't waste any time. She sucks on me and bobs her head up and down, running her lips and tongue along my length. It feels absolutely amazing and for a moment, I forget I'm still on the phone. That is at least until I hear a voice in my ear.

"Mr. Waters?" the voice says. I ignore it. Where the hell is it even coming from? "Mr. Waters, are you still there?"

"Yes," I say when I realize the voice I can hear is coming from the telephone that I'm still holding up to my ear and it belongs to Greta. "I'm here."

Ros chooses that moment to start moving her fist in time with her bobbing head and I gasp.

"Are you ok?" Greta asks.

"Yes," I manage to say.

"Ok. Mr. Mikaelson will take your call. I'm transferring you now," she says.

"Actually Greta, something has come up," I say. "I'm sorry, but I'll have to call back later."

I grip the arm of my chair until my knuckles whiten as Ros gives me no reprieve. I am so close to coming and I try my best to hold back, aware that I'm still on the phone to a client and too professional to hang up on her.

"Ok," Greta says. "But I can't guarantee he'll still be here."

"That's ok. If he's not, he can call me at his convenience," I say.

My voice breaks on the last word, and I hang up the phone quickly in case Greta has anything else to say. I close my eyes and lean my head back against the headrest on my chair, finally able to relax and enjoy the warmth of Ros's mouth on my cock. Trying to hold myself back has only made me feel even more turned on and it's only a couple more minutes until I spurt into Ros's mouth. She swallows my seed and keeps sucking and swallowing, drinking me dry of every last drop of my cum.

"Holy shit Ros, that was fucking amazing," I say as Ros gets up, wiping a stray bit of my cum from her chin.

"I aim to please," she says with a grin.

"Oh, you sure did that," I tell her.

"It was really good timing too," Ros says with a cheeky smile. "Catching you on the phone like that."

"I really shouldn't encourage that kind of behavior, but trying to act normal on the phone actually made it hotter," I admit to her.

"You did a good job of it to be fair," she says.

"Maybe next time I can even speak to the client," I say.

"Next time?" Ros says.

"Well, you were so good at the task, I thought I might make it one of your regular duties," I say.

"Did you now?" Ros says with a grin.

I nod.

"Yes. But I think it might be a better idea if you get under the desk from now on, just in case someone does come in. It's ok just saying don't tell them to come in, but if they think I'm not here and they only want to leave something for me to look at, they might come in to put it on my desk," I say.

"Honestly Alex, do you think I'd risk getting caught doing that in the middle of the afternoon to my boss? I was mortified when a cleaner almost saw us kissing outside of work hours. I told Will I had something private to discuss with you and not to let anyone in," Ros says.

I laugh and shake my head at her. I really should have known she had done something like that.

"While you're here, I do actually want to ask you something," I say. "Something non- work related. You can say no if you want to without any hard feelings. But I was wondering if you would like to be my plus one for my cousin's birthday party this Saturday night?"

"I'd love to," Ros says, smiling at me.

"Perfect," I say. "I'm looking forward to it already."

CHAPTER
Eighteen
ROS

I'm wearing a cream-colored dress that sits just above my knee. On top of the dress is a layer of silvery chiffon with a dusky pink rose pattern on it. The cream-colored lining stops just above my bust and the chiffon carries on a little bit higher and also creates two short sleeves. I've paired the dress with a pair of silver strappy sandals that lace up my legs, and a silver clutch bag. My hair is all pinned up, and I'm wearing a silver bracelet and necklace, and I reach up to my ear and insert a silver hoop earring. I put the other one in and check my reflection in the mirror. I'm good to go, and I spritz myself in Mademoiselle perfume and head out of my room.

I'm ready a little bit early, and Fiona isn't home, so I have no one to talk to. I go to the kitchen and pour myself a small glass of rose wine from an open bottle in the fridge and then I go to the living room and sit and sip it.

I'm looking forward to tonight; the music, the dancing, the laughter, and the chance to enjoy all of those things with Alex. Even though Alex and I work well together now, it will be nice to catch up with Mr. Waters too. He's bound to be there because it's Alex's cousin's party. That's when I realize something. When Alex said I wasn't under any pressure to say yes to this and he would understand if I didn't want to go, I didn't really give it much thought at the time. But now I can see what he meant; me going to the party with Alex is a pretty strong statement to his family that we are a couple, and of course, that includes Mr. Waters. Alex was letting me know that if I'm not ready for Mr. Waters to think we're together, that I was ok to just say so.

I debate for a moment how I feel about it and I'm pleased to discover I don't mind him knowing about us. And the fact that Alex recognizes what a big step this is and invited me anyway must mean he's at least fairly serious about me. I'm so happy about this development, because it's fair to say I am falling fast for Alex and it's good to have some indication that he is, if not there yet, at least on the right path to falling for me too. The idea gives me a warm glow in my stomach, and I can't even blame the glass of wine I drank because it was too small to affect me like this. No, the warm glow is definitely all about Alex.

The intercom buzzes and I get up and go and answer it.

"It's me," Alex says.

"I'm on my way," I tell him,

I already have money and my cell phone in my clutch bag, so I get my keys from the hook beside the door and step outside, closing and locking the door behind me. I put the keys in my clutch bag with my other things and head down to the lobby and outside where Alex waits for me curbside alongside a black town car. He smiles as I approach him.

"You look beautiful," he says. "As always."

"You scrub up ok yourself," I say with a smile.

He's wearing black jeans and a white, short sleeved, button-down shirt that makes him look tanned and shows off his toned arms. He looks so good I almost tell him to forget the party and just come upstairs with me while we have the place to ourselves. I refrain though and when Alex opens the door of the car and gestures for me to get in, I thank him and get in. I slide over and he gets in next to me and closes the door.

"Just to the venue now please Will," he says.

"Oh, hi Will," I say. "I didn't realize that was you."

"Good evening," Will says, and then he pulls away and heads toward the Fairmont, the hotel where the party is taking place in one of their function rooms.

The hotel isn't that far from my building, and we soon pull up outside of it. Alex picks up a pink gift bag and gets out of his side of the car and I go to open my own door, but Will beats me to it. I thank him and get out and he closes the door behind me. The three of us head to the entrance of the hotel where Will hands the keys to the valet and takes the ticket from him.

"I've already been and scouted out the function room," Will says to Alex as we head inside. "There is the main entrance obviously, and the only other door leads to a fenced in terrace. I have a man situated at the gate to the terrace and I'll be staying in place by the main door."

"Thanks, Will," Alex says.

Will nods to him and then falls into place, his standard four or five steps behind us. Alex offers me his arm and I link my hand through his elbow, and he leads me to the function room. We enter through a set of white double doors decorated with small glass panels that give a peep into the room but not enough to really see much of anything. Will remains behind and Alex and I step into the room.

The tables and chairs are covered in white covers with red runners on the tables and red ribbons around the chairs. Silver balloons dance in the center of each table, and over by the dance floor where the cake is displayed, there's a large silver and red balloon arch. The music is playing quietly in the background for now to allow the guest of honor to greet her friends and family as they arrive.

Alex leads me toward a pretty brunette with long curls and wearing a red dress. She squeals with excitement as she sees Alex and they hug.

"I'm so glad you made it," she says.

"How could I miss my baby cousin's thirty-fifth birthday?" Alex says.

He hands the gift bag to her, and she thanks him. He gestures to me.

"Jenny, this is Ros, my girlfriend. Ros, this is Jenny, my cousin and one time partner in crime," Alex says.

The word girlfriend makes my skin tingle and my stomach roll gently. Alex and I haven't really had a conversation about that yet, but we are exclusive, we did establish that much, and I suppose it's better than describing me as the girl he's fucking. Still though, it feels nice to have him claim me as his like that.

I start to lift my hand to shake Jenny's hand, but she comes in for a hug like she's known me all her life. I return the hug, which I feel should be awkward, but somehow, it isn't. We release each other and smile as Jenny holds me out at arm's length and looks at me.

"I'm so excited to meet you," she says. She playfully slaps Alex's arm. "You kept this quiet."

"I'm not one to brag," Alex says and both Jenny and I make matching snorting noises and then we both laugh.

"I see you've got him figured out," she says to me. And then to Alex. "I like her. She's a keeper."

"I know," Alex replies.

"Does Grandad know?" Jenny says and Alex shakes his head. She grins and turns around and shouts across the room. "Grandad, come and meet Alex's girlfriend."

This is it then. The moment Mr. Waters finds out about

Alex and me. I hope he takes it well, and if he isn't happy, I really hope he doesn't spoil Jenny's night because of it. Mr. Waters appears at Jenny's side.

"Grandad, this is-" Jenny starts.

"Ros," Mr. Waters finishes for her, pulling me into a hug. "How good to see you again."

"Wait, you knew?" Jenny says.

"That they are together? No," Mr. Waters says. "But I've known Ros for a long time. She used to be my personal assistant."

"It looks like she's taking the title personal, even more seriously with Alex," Jenny says. She instantly looks mortified and puts her hand over her mouth. "Oh my God, sorry Ros, I didn't mean that how it sounded."

We're all laughing, and I shake my head at her apology.

"It's ok," I say. "Really."

"How have you been Mr. Waters?" I ask.

"I think you can call me Evan now, we're practically family," Evan says, and I blush and smile.

"Ok," I agree.

"And in answer to your question, I've been good. Better than good. I've been on a cruise and a hiking tour of Somatra since I left work. All with a beautiful woman by my side who shares my love of adventure and travel."

"That's great to hear," I say, meaning it.

"So do we get to meet this special lady?" Alex asks.

"Sure. Come on over," Evan says.

We exchange 'catch you later' messages with Jenny who is rushing off to greet more guests anyway and then we follow Evan back to his table where a woman sits beaming at us. She's thin, but she looks strong, not frail. She has long white hair that she's wearing in a French plait, and she's wearing a peach-colored blouse with white cotton trousers. She looks lovely and I would never have believed her to be in her eighties if I hadn't already known.

"Irene, this is my grandson Alex and his girlfriend, Ros. Ros, Alex, this is Irene," Evan says.

"His girlfriend," Irene says with a twinkle in her eye.

I decide I'm going to like Irene.

"Join us won't you," Evan says after we have exchanged greetings with Irene. Alex looks at me to confirm I want to, and I nod and we take the spare seats at the table. I sit beside Evan facing Alex and he sits beside Irene. "Let me get us a round of drinks. Alex, Ros, what would you like?"

Alex asks for a rum and coke, and I ask for a vodka and orange and Evan goes toward the bar. When he's out of ear shot, Irene smiles at us.

"Well, it seems he was right, although I suppose he had to be one way or the other," she says, smiling fondly after Evan. She turns toward Alex and me. "The day he came in to do the final handover, I was waiting for him to go for lunch afterward and he said to me his grandson and his personal assistant had chemistry and they would either kill each other or fall in love with each other."

"Don't be too hasty," I say. "Killing him isn't off the table yet."

Irene and I laugh, and Alex shakes his head.

"See what I have to put up with Irene?" he says.

CHAPTER
Nineteen

ROS

The conversation is paused as a man approaches us and Alex gets up and embraces him. He introduces me to him, and I discover he's Jenny's brother and another one of Alex's childhood pals. The two cousins are the ones who Evan always used to take to the theme park with him.

The next few hours pass over in a blur of introductions, laughter, the buffet and then the cake cutting and Jenny's speech, and my particular favorite, stories of Alex as a child. By the time the music gets started properly and people older than ten are up and dancing, I have pretty much forgotten who is who already, there have been that many people. I have Evan and Irene memorized obviously, plus Jenny and her brother and a few other people stick in my mind such as Jenny's mom who was the sister of Alex's father.

One thing I do notice which I really like is that the family all seems really close. They laugh and joke around together and everyone seems to know everyone else well enough to have plenty of inside jokes. They are a warm and welcoming bunch and for all I've forgotten a lot of their names, I feel like I've known them all of my life.

"Come on," Michael, Jenny's brother, says as he stops by our table and takes my hand. "Let's dance."

I let him pull me to my feet and lead me to the dance floor and we spin and dance and laugh together to Meatloaf's Bat Out of Hell and then Taylor Swift's Shake It Off. Jenny and some of her friends have dragged Alex up too and even Evan and Irene are up and dancing.

The next song starts, and Alex comes over to Michael and me.

"Sorry man, I need to steal my girl," he says.

Michael does a little bow and laughs and backs away and Alex takes me in his arms, and we move around the dance floor. We dance together and as the song comes to a close, Alex leans down and kisses me. I wrap my arms around his shoulders and kiss him back, swaying to the music as the next song starts up. He holds me around my waist and our bodies press close together and for a moment, it feels like we are the only two people in the world.

Finally, we break apart and go back to dancing. Jenny joins us for a while and some of her friends do too. We only stop dancing for long enough to drink our drinks and then we're up and moving again. I'm surprised when the bartender calls for any last orders as I had no idea the night was so close to being over.

Alex goes to the bar and gets a last round in for us and Evan and Irene and then we take to the dance floor for one last song. The DJ has slowed it right down and Alex and I dance in each other's arms. It is only when the song is almost finished that I feel eyes on me and I see Gloria, one of the accountants from work, sitting at a table at the edge of the dance floor. She sees me looking in her direction and smiles and waves and I return the gesture.

"What's she doing here?" I ask Alex, mortified that someone from work has seen us together like this.

He shrugs his shoulders.

"I have no idea," he says. "She must either be a friend of Jenny's or someone's plus one."

I force myself to stop worrying about Gloria's presence. I don't want to ruin what has otherwise been a lovely night. The song ends and the lights come up, and despite me not wanting to focus on Gloria, I have to admit I'm glad to be going back to our table away from her line of sight.

We finish up our last drinks and say our goodbyes to Evan and Irene who announce their cab has arrived.

"I've texted Will to get our car," Alex says after typing on his cell phone.

We go and find Jenny and say goodnight to her and wish her a happy birthday again. She thanks us for coming, saying how she has had a lovely time and how we should all meet up at some point for a night out or something, something which Alex and I readily agree to. I really like Jenny and I'd love to get to know her better.

We go outside and get into the waiting car which takes us to Alex's place. We go inside.

"Do you want a night cap?" Alex asks.

I shake my head.

"If it's all the same to you, I'd rather go straight up to bed," I say.

"I hope you don't mean to sleep," Alex says, playfully pinching my ass.

"I'm sure you can find a way to keep me awake," I say.

"You know it," Alex says, and I start up the stairs and he follows behind me.

We take a turn each in the bathroom where I unpin my hair, wash my makeup off and brush my teeth with a spare toothbrush Alex has assigned to me at his place. I pee and then I take my dress and underwear and shoes off and go through to the bedroom. Alex is already in bed, his lamp casting the only light in the room.

"Wow," Alex says as I step into the lit part of the room as I head toward the bed. "You looked great in that dress, but I have to say you look even better out of it."

"You charmer," I say, getting into bed beside Alex and laying down to face him.

He cups my cheek with his hand and leans in and kisses me full on the lips. He tastes of minty toothpaste, and I can smell his cologne and the manly smell of him beneath it. I wrap my arm around him and pull him closer to me. I love that he is all man and that he is all mine.

We keep kissing and I hook my leg over Alex's hips and rub my lips over his cock. It instantly hardens and he sucks in air through his teeth as he kisses down my neck. I shift the angle of my hips and then I reach down and grab Alex's cock and push it against my pussy opening. He takes the hint and thrusts into me, spreading me open and filling me up.

"Oh Alex," I moan as we start to thrust against each other. His cock rubs over my g-spot at this angle and each thrust is like a mini orgasm as the intense sensation pulses through me.

He thrusts into me until I'm barely able to function as the pleasure rips through my body but never quite hits the climax I need to reach to release me from this delicious torment. My fingers dig into Alex's back as I gasp for air and try to grind myself harder against him.

"Oh God Alex, please let me come," I moan.

"I'll see what I can do," he says and grins at me and then his mouth is on mine and his tongue is in my mouth, probing and swirling and still he teases me, his cock rubbing over my g-spot time and time again until I really don't think I can take it anymore.

Alex finally pushes me onto my back and rolls with me, staying inside of me. He pulls his mouth from mine and looks down at me. I look deep into his eyes as he thrusts all the way inside of me, stretching my pussy and making me gasp. He keeps thrusting, long and hard and then he speeds up, and rubs his fingers over my nipples, first one and then the other one.

"Come for me," he says, and as he speaks, he pushes his hand down between our writhing bodies and presses down on my already swollen clit.

Pleasure explodes through me and for a moment, my vision goes black as I try and fail to suck in air. My back arches and my pussy tightens itself around Alex's cock. I dig my nails into his shoulders and as I manage to drag in a breath, I practically scream his name as another wave of pleasure cascades over my body.

My orgasm slowly fades, leaving me feeling warm and sated and I pull Alex's face down to mine and kiss him tenderly. He kisses me back and then he thrusts into me once more and this time, it's his turn to orgasm. His face twists in ecstasy as his body freezes and he spurts into me. Only his cock moves, spasms of pleasure making it feel almost like it's vibrating inside of me.

"Ah fuck," Alex calls out and then he slumps down on top of me, spent and panting. I wrap my arms around him, and he stays there for a moment and then he rolls off me and lays down beside me.

When I have my breath back, I roll toward him, and he lifts his arm up for me. I snuggle closer and rest my head on his shoulder and he wraps his arm around me. I put my arm on his belly, my palm flat on his chest. He's still getting his breath back and my hand moves up and down with his panting.

"Thank you," I say. "For tonight I mean. I had a great time. Your family is really nice."

"They are if they like someone. You made a good impression," he says.

"Well, that's good to know," I say.

"The party was fun, but the best part of the night happened right here," he says.

"And that part doesn't need to be over yet," I say.

My pussy feels bruised and my clit aches, but I know that one touch from Alex would make me want to go again and forget the aches and pains.

"Give me a few minutes to get my breath back," Alex says.

We fall silent and I trace a circle on Alex's chest with one finger. It's nice just laying here in his arms like this. I think he must have gotten his breath back by now though because his breathing has slowed right down. That's when I realize that he seems to have fallen asleep. He takes a deep breath that ends in a snore, and I know I was right.

"Hey," I say, lifting my head from his shoulder. "I thought it was me who needed help staying awake."

He opens one eye.

"What can I say? You wore me out," he says.

His voice is thick and slurred with sleep and his eye has closed again before he has even finished speaking. I need to wake him up before he gets into a deep sleep if I'm to get what I want from him tonight. I kiss his neck, but he doesn't seem to notice so I kiss up it and lightly run my lips across his. His lips part slightly, and I think he's waking up, but then he snores again.

"Alex," I say. "Time to wake up."

"Mm," he says and then he mutters something that I can't make out and goes back to snoring.

I sigh and lay my head back on his shoulder, accepting the fact I'm not going to be able to get him awake enough to fuck me all night. Oh well. He can make it up to me tomorrow I think to myself with a grin.

I lay next to him, letting the rhythm of his quiet snores and the up and down movement of his chest lull me into sleep with him.

CHAPTER
Twenty
ROS

I had half forgotten about Gloria being at Jenny's party until I step out of my car in the work parking lot on Monday morning. I wonder if she's said anything to anyone. I know some of the people in the office love to gossip, but I have no idea if Gloria is one of them. I don't really know her that well, but I know she's an accountant, so maybe she's a bit more discrete and cleverer than the average person here and maybe then she's above spreading gossip about her coworkers. At least I hope that's the case.

I enter the building and cross the lobby, passing a good morning to the receptionist there. I get in the elevator and hit the button for the fourth floor. I'm feeling pretty good when the doors open and I step out onto the fourth floor, but then I see one of the receptionists there nudging another one and they both look at me and my good feeling falls away. They know. It's obvious that they know. I guess Gloria is a gossip after all.

"I take you had a good weekend Ros," Celia says with a sickly-sweet smile that I want to smack off her face.

"Perfect thank you," I say. "How about you?"

"All good," she says. "What did you do?"

The other receptionists snicker and I choose to ignore them and rise above it.

"I went to a party on Saturday night, and then I spent most of Sunday lazing about in bed and recovering from my hangover," I say.

"Sounds like a fun Sunday," one of the others, I don't catch which one, whispers.

"It was, thank you," I say and when I see Estelle's cheeks going red, I know it was her who spoke and that I wasn't really meant to hear her. "Anyway, duty calls. Catch you later ladies."

I get a few mumbled responses as I walk away. I'm dying to look back, knowing I'll see the pack of bitches in a little huddle whispering about me and giggling, but I won't give them the satisfaction of catching them in the act and looking upset about it. I will simply rise above it. Or at least act like that's what I'm doing.

I'm ever so grateful that my desk is hidden away for the most part. It will be my sanctuary today, tucked away in the back where no one will see or talk to me. I reach my desk and I feel better straight away when I see Will in place outside of Alex's office. Knowing Alex is here too and we're in this together relaxes me a touch and I decide to go and see if he has had to deal with anything similar. I seriously doubt he has though – surely no one is going to have been stupid enough to tease the boss.

"Morning," I say to Will as I tap on Alex's office door.

"Morning Ros," he says.

I debate asking Will if anyone has said anything to him about us, but I don't want him to think I'm a paranoid wreck. Besides, it seems most people here find it much easier than I do to accept Will as a background fixture and not really talk to him or acknowledge that he's there.

Alex calls for me to come in and I open his office door and slip inside and close the door behind me.

"They know," I say.

"What?" Alex says.

"They know," I repeat.

"I heard you," Alex says.

"Then why did you say what?" I ask.

"I meant what as in who knows what?" he says.

I'm pacing his floor in front of his desk, and I shake my head and sigh.

"Ros, are you ok? Why don't you sit down?" Alex says.

I shake my head more noticeably and wave away his concern.

"I'm fine. And I don't want to sit down. It's out. About us. Everyone knows we're a thing," I say.

"Is that really so bad?" Alex says. "Are you that ashamed of the idea of being with me?"

"What? No, of course not," I say. "I just hate being the subject of office gossip. I came in this morning and the receptionists had a good laugh at my expense. Fucking Celia asking what I'd done all weekend while the others giggled behind her."

"I'm sure Celia was just making conversation and not trying to embarrass you," Alex says.

I resist the urge to roll my eyes. I forgot Alex won't have a bad word said about Celia. I need to pick my battles wisely though and that's a fight for another day. Right now, I'm more concerned with everyone in the building discussing my private life.

"Maybe," I say. "But there's no denying the others were giggling and whispering."

"It kind of shows how boring their own lives are if ours is that interesting to them," Alex says.

"I don't care how boring their lives are. I don't want mine

being a topic of conversation," I say. I narrow my eyes at him. "You don't seem to be particularly upset about this."

"Honestly Ros, I'm not. I don't care what anyone else thinks as long as we're happy. It's obvious you aren't happy at the minute though. There's not much I can do to stop the gossip entirely, but I can make a show of where I stand on it and hopefully calm it down a bit," he says.

"That's better than nothing, I guess. How will you do that?" I stop pacing and face Alex.

"The gossip had to have started with Gloria. I'll fire her and make an example of her, and the others might learn to keep their mouths shut," Alex says.

I shake my head and resume pacing the ground.

"No. You can't do that," I say.

"Sure, I can. I'm the CEO, remember?" Alex says.

"I don't mean you can't physically do it. I mean it's not right. I don't want to see someone lose their career over this," I say.

"Ok, I won't fire her. But I can't see what else could work. Even if I pull her aside and have words with her, the rumor is out there now and it won't stop because I tell Gloria off for starting it," Alex says.

"I guess I'll just have to get used to being talked about," I say.

"Just remember Ros. You were here in this exact role long before I came along. No one can say you got your job by sleeping with the boss," he says.

I consider this for a moment and realize it is of course true. I feel better about that. As long as no one thinks I'm getting any sort of advantages at work in exchange for sexual favors, I don't really care if they talk about me. That level of gossip is no different than if Gloria had seen me with a handsome stranger and told people I was seeing someone. And I would have just laughed along with that kind of talk.

"You're right," I say. "And I know just how to stop all of this."

"What are you going to do?" Alex asks, looking at me suspiciously.

"Nothing bad," I say. "I'm just going to stop letting the gossip get to me and stop denying it and they'll get bored eventually."

Alex nods his head.

"Sounds like a plan," he says.

I smile and leave his office and head back toward my desk. I go to sit down, but then I decide against it, and instead, I head back toward the elevators. I might as well do this now rather than later and get it over with. I go down to the lobby and sit down for a few minutes and then I come back up and step back out of the elevator onto our floor again.

"I forgot my cell phone in my car," I say, rolling my eyes as I approach the desk. "I swear I'm getting worse as I get older."

I did no such thing of course and if any of them were paying attention, they'd have seen that I didn't have my cell phone in my hand, nor do I have any pockets. But they are much more focused on other things, as I knew they would be. Other things like who I may or may not have slept with on Saturday night.

"Selena has something to ask you," Estelle says.

I smile sweetly at Selena who blushes and shakes her head.

"No, I don't," she says.

"Don't be shy. I don't bite," I say, but Selena shakes her head and refuses to look away from her screen. Estelle sighs.

"Fine. I'll ask her then," she says. "Someone told us that you bumped into Alex at a party on Saturday night. And that you kissed him on the dance floor."

"That's not a question," I say, forcing myself to sound

casual even though I want to slap Estelle's face for this. And Celia's face. Even Selena's face. For all Selena refused to embarrass me by questioning me, she still obviously has been part of the conversation about me.

"Is it true?" Estelle says. "That's my question."

"No," I say. "I didn't bump into Alex at a party. I was there as his plus one."

"Wait. You two are…?" Estelle says, trailing off.

"Dating?" I say, filling in her pause with a smile. "Yes."

"Oh, you lucky thing, he's gorgeous," Estelle says.

"I bet he knows how to treat a woman too," Selena puts in.

"All I'm going to say on the matter is that I am extremely happy," I say with a wink that makes the two women giggle and Celia glare at me. Celia's glare makes me say something I hadn't planned on. "And I am definitely satisfied if you know what I mean."

This gets another round of giggles, and I'm laughing with them as I walk away, giving them a 'see you later' over my shoulder as I go.

I'm pleased with myself as I reach my desk and get back to work. I have taken back the power by stopping the rumor being something to debate and whisper about. It's out there now. Alex and I are dating and the whole firm knows about it.

"Did your plan work then?" Alex asks as we sit in his car headed to his place for dinner after work that day.

"Yes," I say. "I'm actually shocked at how quickly it did the trick. I had a few people ask me if it was true we are dating and when I said yes, that was it. Already the receptionists are gossiping about Kayleigh and who she supposedly likes."

"Who?" Alex asks.

"Ugh. I thought you were meant to be above office gossip," I say.

He shrugs his shoulders.

"I am meant to be. But I'm still allowed to be curious right?" he says.

"Scott. From IT," I say. "But I'm not saying there's any truth to it."

"Maybe there isn't. But it seems like it's easier to get the people off your back if it's true because denying it only seems to make them worse," Alex says.

"That's it exactly. The best thing Kayleigh can do is either admit if it's true or lie and admit it even if it's not true."

"Would you have lied about us if we weren't seeing each other, and the rumor started?" Alex asks.

"I probably would have said just enough to convince them they were right without coming right out and saying it. It's weird because if it wasn't true I wouldn't have been half as bothered about the rumor," I say.

"I don't think I'll ever fully understand these office politics," Alex says, shaking his head.

"That's probably for the best. They're crazy," I say with a laugh. "And besides, that's part of the reason why you have a personal assistant, so you don't have to get your hands dirty getting any gossip you want passed along."

"Not me," Alex says, shaking his head. "I had my moment of curiosity and it's gone. Mostly because I don't really care one way or the other whether Kayleigh really likes Scott or not, and I guess gossip is a bit boring when you don't care about the outcome."

"It is," I agree.

"The only outcome I'm concerned with is ours," Alex says. "And I don't need Gloria or anyone else to tell me that it's going well, and I've never been happier."

I smile at him, a warm glow spreading through me at his words. He's never been happier. That makes two of us and I start to find the words to tell Alex I feel the same, but he starts talking about something else and the moment passes. It doesn't change how I feel though, and I am practically walking on air when we reach Alex's place and go inside.

CHAPTER
Twenty-One
ROS

It's been a few months since everyone at Waters Financial found out that Alex and I are dating. It's been a really good few months for us too. We are still really happy together, and although we don't officially live together, I find that I'm spending more and more time at Alex's place and that more and more of my stuff is ending up there. I even have my own section of the closet and my own drawer at his place.

We've been all over together, including a repeat visit to the theme park we visited before, this time with Jenny and Michael and Evan and Irene as a surprise like I suggested. Evan absolutely loved it and we even managed to convince them to go on a couple of rides. They chose the gentle options – the bumper cars and the carousel, but it was still so good to see them enjoying themselves. We've also been to a family barbecue thrown by Jenny's mom, and I really feel like I'm being accepted by his lovely family.

Fiona has started dating a guy named Luke and we've been on a few double dates with them, and I know Alex has grown on Fiona a lot as she has spent time in our company and seen how well he treats me.

Just last week, Alex and I had a weekend away together and it was so nice just to relax and sightsee and be together like that. Of course, reality had to hit, and we had to come back home and back to work but it was lovely while it lasted.

Work is going as well as our relationship. We have successfully integrated Lance's new company into his account and the company's revenue has gone through the roof, meaning that we are now on more company's radars which means that in turn, we are getting even more clients. Alex has had to take on even more accountants than he originally thought he would need to, just to keep up with the growing demands.

It kind of feels like it's all too good to be true and if everything was completely perfect, I would be waiting for the other shoe to drop and something to go wrong, but as it stands, it's not completely perfect. There is one little annoyance that can't be shaken off – Celia and her attitude toward me. Whenever she interacts with me in front of Alex or Will, she acts like we're best friends. Even in front of other staff she is friendly enough to me, but when it's only me and her, her claws come out and she is a total bitch to me.

I can't say I'm particularly upset by Celia's obvious dislike of me, although it does bug me why she hates me so much and why she seemed to have already decided she was going to hate me before we even met. I tried to ask Alex about it once, but he told me I was being silly, that she was likely just joking around and I had to get to know her a bit more to fully understand her humor. I haven't bothered trying to tell him what she's really like since then because I don't want him to think I'm paranoid, or worse, jealous of her because she's friends with him.

If Celia being an asshole to me is the worst thing in my

life, I still call that winning, and if that's the price to pay for everything else in my life to be going so well, I'm more than happy to continue to pay it.

My desk phone rings, bringing me out of my daydream and I answer it. It's someone from reception needing me to authorize an order for stationery that they have sent through to me. I check my email and see it there.

"I'll have a look now," I say. "Give me two minutes."

I hang up the phone and open the email. I quickly open the attached order and scan through the requested items. It all seems to be reasonable and in order and so I sign it off as authorized and send it back to the reception inbox. I reach for my desk phone to call them and let them know it's done, but as my hand hovers over the receiver, ready to pick it up, an email pings back into my inbox from the team thanking me.

I'm ready to move onto my next task and I minimize my emails and open up a new tab. I haven't gotten any further than that when Alex comes out of his office and comes over to my desk.

"Come and have lunch with me," he says.

"I'll eat later," I say. "I want to get this report finished first."

"What's the deadline for it?" he says.

"The end of the day," I tell him. "But it's my own personal target to finish it before I take a lunch break."

I grin at him, knowing he gets a kick out of my little quirks, but he doesn't smile back, and my own smile starts to fade away. Alex shakes his head.

"No. This is more important. Come on, I need to talk to you about something," he says.

"Can we not talk in your office?" I ask.

"It's a personal matter," he says. "Now for God's sake, stop questioning me and come on."

I can feel a pit of worry in my stomach. Whatever it is he

wants to talk to me about, it seems pretty serious for him to be this stern with me. And it's personal so I'm not in trouble from work. What the hell is going on here? I guess there's one way to find out, because Alex obviously isn't willing to discuss it here. I reach down between my feet and get my purse then I lock my computer and stand up.

"Let's go," I say.

I wait until we're out of the office and in the street and then I turn to Alex.

"What's this all about?" I ask.

"I told you I need to talk to you about something. Not here though. Once we're sitting down somewhere comfortably and we can talk properly I'll tell you," he says.

He's still being kind of stern, but he doesn't seem angry with me, and although I'm nervous still, I decide to just stop asking questions and wait to see what this is about. It's probably nothing and I'm just worrying myself for the sake of it.

I quietly follow Alex to a café we often visit on our lunch break. The waitress sees us come in and smiles at us. We greet her and she takes us to our usual table, which is toward the back of the room. It was a table we chose when we were still trying to keep our relationship on the down low, and now it will serve a good purpose as somewhere to talk without being overheard.

"The usual?" the waitress asks us, and I nod. Alex thinks for a moment and then he does the same. We make our way to our table and by the time we've gotten settled down and Alex has taken his jacket off, the waitress is bringing us our drinks – Coke for me, sparkling water for Alex.

I can already see the girl behind the counter making our sandwiches so when the waitress walks away, I nod toward her.

"We might as well wait until we get our food then we can talk without being disturbed," I say.

Alex nods his head in agreement and a silence falls between us. Instead of the usual comfortable silence we have between us, this one feels kind of heavy and I can't handle it. It makes me feel anxious and I hate feeling like that. I get up quickly.

"I'm going to the bathroom," I say.

CHAPTER
Twenty-Two
ROS

I move across the place and go upstairs where the bathrooms are. I don't need to go so I move to the sinks and wash my hands for something to do. I wait long enough that I hope the sandwiches will be there and Alex can tell me what the hell is going on and then hopefully, I can laugh at myself for blowing this thing all out of proportion.

I go back down the stairs and as I reach the bottom, I glance through the glass door into the street. Will is stationed beside the door and pedestrians hurry back and forth along the street. It's just a normal day, yet I still feel like something ominous is hanging over me as I head back to our table. I'm relieved to see our sandwiches there. Thank God for small mercies.

I sit back down at the table.

"Are you alright?" Alex asks me and I force a smile and nod.

I pick my sandwich up and take a bite. It's delicious as always, chicken and stuffing on a soft white bun. Alex has his standard cheese and ham baguette. He's already started in on it while I was in the bathroom.

"Well?" I say, sick of waiting now.

"I need to ask you something important, and I need you to swear you will answer me honestly," Alex says.

Ok, this isn't so bad. Whatever it is he thinks I've done, I can honestly say I haven't, because I know I haven't done anything to make him act this way. I nod.

"I need you to say it," Alex says.

"Cross my heart and hope to die," I say.

"I'm being serious Ros," Alex says.

"So am I," I tell him. "I'm not in the habit of lying and I don't intend to start now."

Alex nods his head and then he looks me in the eye as he asks his question.

"Is it true you almost did jail time for stabbing someone?" he says.

His question absolutely floors me. It was the last thing I was expecting, and I feel a wave of nausea flood through me. I take a quick gulp of my soda and instantly, my stomach settles back down.

"How the hell do you know about that?" I ask.

"So, it's true then?" Alex says, avoiding my question.

We're going to get nowhere if we both keep just avoiding answering each other's questions, so I decide to just explain things to him. I'm not ashamed of what I did, and I have no problem telling him about it. The only reason I haven't told him yet is because it's just not something that I feel has a bearing on my life choices these days and it's something I don't really think about anymore.

"Yes, it's true. I narrowly avoided going to jail, and instead, I got a suspended sentence and community service," I say. "But there was a reason for what I did. I didn't just wake up one morning and go psycho and stab a stranger for a laugh."

"I didn't think you would have," Alex says. "I'd be interested to hear what actually happened though."

"The guy I stabbed, Danny, he wasn't just some random guy. He was my boyfriend at the time," I say. "We'd been together for about six months and things were great at first. Danny was very sweet, very attentive, and kind of old school, like he'd hold doors open for me that sort of thing. My family loved him, my friends loved him. And then he changed. I can't put my finger on exactly when it happened, because it wasn't just an overnight thing. It was a long, slow process that I didn't notice until it was too late."

"He started verbally abusing me first, putting me down, telling me I was too fat, or that I was ugly or stupid, or any one of a hundred other insults. He would tell me I was lucky to be with him because no one else would have me, and I was young and stupid, and I started to believe him. He managed to stop me seeing most of my family and friends. He used excuses to them, saying I was depressed and didn't want to see anyone and all this crap. Most of them bought it and thought he was the most amazing boyfriend, helping me through this dark period. Only Fi saw through it, and she would regularly turn up on my doorstep to see me, only to be turned away by Danny, who at that point, had pretty much moved in with me without us even discussing it."

"One night, he started on his usual abusive speech, and I don't know why that night was different, but I argued back with him. I thought maybe that would stop things, but it didn't. That was the first time he hit me. I remember it like it was yesterday. He gave me a backhanded slap across the face. My cheekbone was painful and bruised for days."

"Afterward, of course, he was all apologies, and I was so beaten down by then, so sure he was right about me being fat and ugly and stupid and undeserving of love that I forgave him. At first, things went back to how they used to be, and I saw a glimmer of hope that the old Danny was back. But it didn't last long, and before long, I was getting a beating pretty much daily."

"I figured he would go too far and kill me one day, and I didn't care. Hell, I even wished for it. But then one night, I was making dinner. I had a knife in my hand cutting up a roast and Danny told me I was cutting the slices of meat too thick. He came up behind me and punched me in the side of the head, and something just snapped inside of me. Instead of cringing away from him, I turned to face him and without even thinking what I was doing, I thrust out with the knife. It went between his ribs, and I felt it sliding into his flesh and I saw the fear in his eyes, and in that moment, I knew he was a coward and that I would never ever let anyone treat me that way again."

"It took a while to build my self-worth back up, especially when most of my family took Danny's side, but ultimately, I learned my worth and while I'm not exactly proud of what I did, like I said earlier, I'm not ashamed either."

When I was talking, I felt like I was back there, seeing the moments play out in front of me, a watcher rather than a player, and now, I come to and the café around me comes back into focus, Alex too as he sits across from me, a look of horror on his face.

I feel a tear running down my own face and I reach up and wipe it away, waiting for Alex to speak. His reaction to this will tell me everything I need to know about him.

"Oh my God Ros, I'm so sorry you went through all of that," he says and a part of me relaxes. That was the kind of answer I was looking for. The kind where he realizes that I am the victim not Danny. But I also feel a deep, burning anger at Alex. He has gone snooping into my past, checking up on me, and because of that, I've had to relive one of the most harrowing things that has ever happened to me.

I shrug and give him a sad smile.

"Me too," I say. I stand up and push my chair back.

"Where are you going?" Alex asks.

"Away from you," I say.

"Away from me? But why? Ros, I get why you did what you did. Hell, I think the bastard got away light for what he did to you," Alex says.

Again, it's the right answer, but he doesn't get why I'm mad at him, and I'm not going to stand here and explain it to him.

"You're a clever boy Alex. Work it out for yourself," I say, and I turn and walk away from him.

"Ros. Ros, wait," he calls after me, but I just keep walking. I know exactly who I need to talk to next to get to the bottom of this, and in the meantime, I don't want to talk to Alex. I know he can't follow me straight away because someone needs to pay for our lunch, so if I hurry, I can avoid him easily enough.

CHAPTER
Twenty-Three
ROS

I step out of the café, still ignoring Alex calling my name. Will is still in place outside of the door as I knew he would be.

"I need to talk to you," I say. "It's important."

"Ok," Will says, his face giving nothing away. I have no idea if he knows what Alex has just spoken to me about or not. Well, obviously he knows about it, but I don't know if he knows that today was the day Alex has chosen to talk to me about what they both know about me. "I can't just walk away from here though, not while I'm working. Wait until we're back at work and I'll come and talk to you once Alex is back in his office."

"OK, thanks," I say, and I turn away and hurry back toward the office.

I don't immediately sit down at my desk. Instead, I go to the bathroom, but I keep the main door open a crack so that I can watch for Alex passing by my desk and going back into his office. I don't have to wait long before I hear him yell 'fuck', no doubt at seeing I'm not at my desk. He goes into his office and slams the door. I wait a minute longer in case he decides to go off looking for me, but the door stays shut and I come out of the bathroom. True to his word, Will sees me and comes over to my desk to talk to me.

"What can I do for you Ros?" Will says as he sits down opposite me.

"You can start by telling me your biggest secret," I say.

Will looks at me, the confusion on his face clear to see.

"Come on. Don't be shy. You know all about me, so let's make it an even playing field," I say.

"What's happened Ros?" Will asks and despite my resolve to remain firm and get him to spill something about himself, I sigh and shake my head as tears come to my eyes. I blink them away quickly.

"Alex asked me about something over lunch. Something from my past. I know you must have done some sort of background check on me, and I don't think it's fair that you know all of my intimate shit when I know nothing about you," I say.

"Of course, I did a background check on you. I wouldn't be doing my job properly if I didn't check you out and make sure you're not some social climber or gold digger. You can be as mad as you like about it, but it's my job to protect Alex and making sure he doesn't get taken for a ride is part of that," Will says.

I have to admire the fact he didn't try to deny looking into my past, and I soften a little bit at his explanation. He must have done this a hundred times and found plenty of women who were just after using Alex for money or fame or whatever the hell else those types of women get out of those deals. I know Will hasn't found anything like that in my past, partly because he hasn't tried to stop Alex from dating me, and partly because I haven't done anything like that. I want him to know for sure that I'm not some gold-digging little tramp though and I lean down and get my purse and get my cell phone out. I tap around until I open up my banking app and I turn it around to show Will.

"The top one is my current account," I say. "The bottom one is an inheritance from my grandmother who died when I was seventeen. I'm allowed to use it for rent, education, that kind of stuff for now, but when I'm thirty, I will get the whole amount released to me. All seven million dollars of it. I'm going to be well off in my own right. So, if there is any doubt in your mind, I don't need Alex's money. I'm about to have my own."

"You don't have to show me this stuff," Will says. "I didn't find any red flags in your background and even before seeing that, I didn't think you were just using Alex. In fact, I think you're really good for him."

"You do?" I say and Will nods his head.

"Yes, I do," he confirms. "And like I say, I found nothing in your background to worry about so there was nothing for me to report to Alex. To be honest, I don't even know if he knows I ran a check on you. It's just something I do as standard when someone new comes into his life and gets closer than an acquaintance level."

"Wait, you didn't give Alex anything on me?" I ask. "You mean you didn't find out about the court case?"

"I found it," Will says. "And I looked into the trial and found out the reasons for it. I admire your strength Ros, but I didn't feel it was my place to tell Alex about that. It was something you could choose to tell him or not, but I knew you didn't pose a danger to him because of that because Alex would never hit you."

I watch Will as he talks, and I believe him. He has no reason to lie to me about giving Alex information he found, because if he was going to lie, then the sensible lie would have been to say he hadn't looked into me at all. But now I'm really confused as to how Alex knew about the court case. I hope it doesn't mean the bastard decided to do some sort of background check on me himself.

"Thank you Will. For being honest," I say.

"Of course," he says. "And if you want that Danny character finished off, just say the word."

I shake my head.

"He's not important enough for me to send anyone after him, but thanks again," I say.

"Anytime," Will says. He starts to get up but then he sits back down again. "When I was ten and my sister was five, our house got broken into and the burglar killed my mom as she tried to protect us. I vowed that day I would never again be so helpless and that's in part what led me to my current career. That's my biggest secret."

He doesn't stay for my reaction; he just gets up and goes back to his usual post at Alex's office door. I wonder if I should go over there and tell him I'm sorry about his mom or at least acknowledge what he said, but I figure if he wanted my feedback, he would have stayed seated. I think he'll be happy to just let the conversation be left unsaid, so that leaves me once more to wonder if Alex had decided to look into my background, and if he had, why now?

I don't have an answer to that question, and I try to push it to one side and get back on with my work. I do need to get that report I was about to work on before lunch finished, and I turn to my computer, open up the report, and start working. I finish it in record timing, because I won't let myself stop because I need to think about something other than Alex and focusing solely on the report gives me that. I email it to the appropriate people and then I decide to check my emails again. Before I can open them up, my desk phone rings. I glance at it and see it's the internal line from Alex's office. I'm so tempted to just ignore it, but I'm still at work and he's my boss and my professionalism won't allow me to let my work suffer because of my personal issues.

"Yes?" I say, answering the phone.

"Can you come in here for a sec please?" Alex says. I don't answer straight away, and he goes on. "It's work-related Ros."

"Then yes," I say.

I hang up the phone and go toward Alex's office. Will stands in his usual place and although I decided not to embarrass him further by talking about his secret, there is one thing I feel he needs to hear.

"It goes no further," I say, and he nods once and that's all we need to say on the matter.

I open Alex's office door and go inside.

"Close the door and sit down please," he says, his voice and face both neutral and giving nothing away.

I wonder if I'm in for a telling off, but I don't think that Alex is childish enough to bring our personal issues into work and find something to tell me off for because of what happened in the café. I do as he asks and then I wait patiently for him to tell me what he needs.

"Why are you mad at me?" he asks.

"This isn't about work at all is it?" I ask. I stand up and start for the door, but Alex gets to it first and blocks it.

"Please Ros, talk to me," he says.

He sounds so dejected that I soften a little bit and I sigh. I suppose the least I can do is tell him why I'm annoyed at him.

"What do you expect Alex? If we're going to be together, then you need to trust me. And that means not going digging into my background. If you want to know something about my past, then ask me about it," I say.

"I want to know everything about you Ros, not because I don't trust you but because I love you," he says.

I wasn't expecting that and my jaw drops.

"I...," I start and then I stop, unsure of what to say next.

"It's ok. You don't have to say it back," Alex says with a smile. "But I hope at some point down the line, you want to."

"I love you too," I say, smiling for the first time since he called me in here. "Of course I do. I was just shocked because it was the last thing I was expecting you to say."

Alex cups my chin in his hand and leans in and kisses me full on the mouth. I kiss him back and my body aches for him, my pussy craving the full feeling I get from him. But it's the middle of the day and we're at work and that isn't going to happen. I pull away and we're both slightly breathless as we look into each other's eyes and smile.

"Will you let me explain?" Alex asks and I nod.

He takes my hand and leads me back to his desk. I sit back down in the same seat I have just left and rather than going around to his usual chair, Alex sits down in the chair beside me.

"I didn't do any sort of background check on you Ros. I swear I didn't," he says. He gets up and walks around his desk and opens his bottom drawer. He pulls out a plain white, A4 sized envelope and hands it to me. "This came this morning with the rest of the mail."

Alex sits down again, and I glance down at the envelope. It's plain and unmarked except for a typed address label with Alex's name and the office's address on it. I open it and pull out a single sheet of newspaper. A glance at the headline is enough to tell me the newspaper is an old one and the article is about me. Someone has gone to a lot of effort to track this down just to send it to Alex.

"Was there a note or anything with it?" I ask.

Alex shakes his head.

"No. Nothing. Just what you have there. I have no idea who it came from or why they've sent it to me. To be honest, I only asked you about it because I was convinced someone has done this as a horrible joke or whatever and I thought someone might be out to get you," he says.

"I mean I'd still have to think someone has it in for me. Why else would someone send you this except to try and break us up?" I ask.

"Maybe someone who stumbled across it without knowing the full story and was afraid you would hurt me?" Alex suggests.

I shake my head.

"That makes no sense. Surely, they'd just speak to you. And this isn't something you'd stumble across without looking for it," I say. "I think it's someone trying to cause trouble between us."

"Well then let's show whoever it is that we are bigger and better than their stupid game and rise above it," Alex says. "What do you say? Am I forgiven?"

"Of course you are," I say.

He leans in and kisses me again and I kiss him back. I meant it about him being forgiven, but something about this whole thing nags at me and I don't think I can let it go as easily as Alex seems to be able to. I want to know who sent this to him and why.

CHAPTER
Twenty-Four
ALEX

I knew I was falling for Ros and falling hard, but it was only when I blurted out yesterday that I loved her that it really hit home to me just how much I've fallen for her. I knew I loved her, but when I said it out loud and it all became real, it hit me that Ros is my life now and I can't imagine being without her. I've been debating asking her to marry me for a few weeks and yesterday showed me that the time is right – why wait?

I can't keep the goofy grin off my face as I lift up the receiver of my desk phone and call the management team reception desk.

"Hi Alex, what can I do for you?" a voice says down the line.

I'm pretty sure it's Estelle, but not sure enough to use her name in case I'm wrong. I'm certain it isn't Celia though and it's her I want to talk to.

"Can you put Celia on please?" I ask.

"Are you sure I can't help?" maybe Estelle, maybe not Estelle asks.

"I'm sure," I say.

There's a bit of rustling which I assume is the sound of the receiver being passed from maybe Estelle maybe not Estelle to Celia.

"Hello," Celia's voice comes down the line.

"Hey," I say. "I need a favor. Can you get away for an hour?"

"You're the boss so if you say I can, then yes I can," she replies.

"Good. Be ready to leave in two minutes," I say and hang up the phone.

It's only once I've completed the call that I realize that Jenny might have been a better choice for this. But Celia has impeccable taste and we're reasonably good friends. Plus, she's here now. I might have to wait hours or even days for Jenny to be able to help me. I know what I'm doing – I'm projecting my doubts about what I'm about to do onto this instead of onto the actual proposal. It's stupid because I don't have doubts as such. I know what I want and there is no doubt in my mind that it's Ros, but I am a bit afraid that she'll say no, especially because we haven't been dating for that long really in the big scheme of things.

I tell myself to stop being negative and I stand up and slip my jacket on. I tap my pocket, making sure my wallet is there. It is. I put my cell phone in my other pocket and leave my office. Ros looks up from her computer when I step out. I head toward her.

"I have to step out for an hour or so," I say. "Hold my calls please. And can we take a rain check on lunch?"

"Sure," Ros says. "Is everything ok?"

I nod.

"Yes. See you soon," I say.

I hurry away before she can ask me any more questions. I can feel her eyes on me as I walk down the hallway, Will behind me. I don't think she will call after me – we're at work and she'll assume this is work related and not question me too much – but I'm still relieved when I turn the corner at the end of the hallway and leave her line of sight and emerge into the reception area. Celia is standing leaning against the reception desk with her coat on and her purse slung over her shoulder.

She looks effortlessly stylish in her navy-blue dress and matching coat, with skyscraper heels that not many women could walk in. I have definitely made the right decision on who should help me choose the best ring for Ros if I want it to be classy.

"Are you ready to leave?" I ask Celia and she nods her head.

"See you in a bit, girls," she says to the others who say their goodbyes to her.

We get into the elevator and go down to the lobby.

"Where are we going then?" Celia asks as I lead her to my car.

"The mall," I say, then I turn my attention to Will. "Just ride with us Will. It will be hard enough finding one parking space, let alone two together."

Will nods his head and the three of us get into my car, Celia in the front with me and Will in the back.

"Why the mall?" Celia asks. "New suit day?"

I look down at myself and frown.

"Are you suggesting my suit is shabby?" I ask.

"No, of course I'm not," Celia says. "You look great like always. I just can't think of what else you might need at the mall that you'd need my help with."

I look away from the road for long enough to flash her an excited grin and then I look back at the road.

"I'm buying an engagement ring," I say.

I spot Will smiling in the rear-view mirror, and I wait for Celia to shriek with excitement or at least crack a smile or something, but she does nothing. She just stares at me, and if anything, she looks annoyed.

"What's wrong?" I ask.

"Nothing," she replies. She finally smiles and I'm sure it's not as forced as it looks. It must just be a trick of the light or something. "I'm just surprised, that's all. You two have only been dating for like five minutes."

"When you know, you know," I say, and this time, Celia's smile looks much more real.

"Yes, that's true," she says. "Wow. Congratulations."

"Don't jinx it," I say. "She might say no yet."

"I highly doubt it," Celia says after snorting down her nose at the idea. She must see the way I'm looking at her as I try to figure out what that snort was all about. "Come on Alex. We both know she's not going to say no."

Is she implying Ros is some sort of gold digger? I don't know but it feels like she is implying something.

"And how do we know that?" I ask.

Celia looks at me like I'm crazy and shakes her head.

"You really haven't noticed the way she looks at you? Alex, she loves you as much as you love her," Celia says, and I smile at her and relax.

I have got to stop assuming the worst here. Of course, Celia doesn't think Ros is a gold digger. They are friends for God's sake. Not close friends necessarily, but friends enough that Celia wouldn't assume badly of Ros.

We reach the mall, and I actually find a parking spot pretty easily, although I was right about how hard it would have been to find two together. We get out of the car and head into the mall. I start to ask Celia questions as we walk.

"Do you think a regular cut or something quirky?" I ask.

"I think you can't go wrong with regular. Something timeless and classic. And let's be honest, we have free reign because Ros wouldn't know the difference between the finest clarity diamond and cubic zirconia," Celia says.

What started out as good advice definitely ended in a barb at Ros, and I know I'm not imagining it this time.

"What the hell is that supposed to mean?" I demand.

"Ros doesn't strike me as the materialistic type," Celia says with a shrug. "I think that she's one of those people who genuinely appreciate the thought behind the gift rather than the price tag of it."

Again, Celia has given me an explanation that shows she's being nice about Ros, but the way she's saying these things tells me otherwise. Her tone is cold, and I know Celia well enough to know when she's being a bitch, and I feel like that's what she's doing here. At the same time, I do think she's right about Ros. She will appreciate what the ring symbolizes rather than how big the diamond is.

We're almost at the jewelers I like when Celia nods down a different area of the mall.

"There's a nice jewelry store down there," she says.

"No there isn't. There's a jewelry store that sells costume jewelry to teenagers," I say.

Celia shrugs as if to say, well yes, exactly.

I sigh. "Cee, do you have some sort of problem with Ros? Just the things you're saying makes it sound like you don't like her very much," I say.

"We're friends, right?" she says, and I nod. "So, I can speak freely?" I nod again. "It's not that I don't like Ros. But I'm just not sure she's right for you. Honestly, I feel like you can do better."

"I don't think for a second I can do better as you put it, and I don't want to. I love Ros," I say.

"Ok, then let's just forget I said anything," Celia says.

I nod and I'm glad when we reach the jewelers. We go

inside and start to look at a few of the rings on display. I point to one I like.

"What about that one?" I ask.

Celia shakes her head.

"It's nice, but it's not for Ros," she says. "It's gold."

I roll my eyes. Here we go again. Is Celia seriously going to imply Ros doesn't even deserve a gold ring? Before I can say anything, she goes on.

"All of the jewelry I've seen Ros wear has been white. That makes me think she isn't a fan of yellow gold. Or even if she doesn't mind it, the ring won't go with any of her other pieces. I think you should look for a ring with a white gold band," she says.

I'm glad I didn't get the chance to bite her head off now because she makes a perfectly reasonable point, and now she's said it, I realize she's right – I've never seen Ros wear yellow gold jewelry either.

"Good idea," I say, and when one of the sales assistants comes over, I ask to see the white gold engagement ring collection.

After looking at lots of different styles, Celia and I agree on a square cut diamond on a beautiful white gold band. I guess Ros's fingers are about the same size as Celia's fingers, so I have her try the ring on to see what size to get. We find the right one and Celia holds her hand out in front of herself, admiring the ring and smiling. She moves her hand this way and that, so that the light bounces off the diamond, making it sparkle even brighter.

"Umm you know that's not for you right?" I say, making it sound like I'm joking although I'm actually quite concerned at how Celia is smiling when she looks at the ring on her finger.

"I am well aware of that," she says, still looking at the

ring. "But that doesn't mean I can't admire its beauty, does it?"

CHAPTER
Twenty-Five
ALEX

After a few more minutes and some obvious throat clearing from the assistant, Celia takes the ring off and lets the assistant box it up, I pay for it, and we leave the store. I can't resist getting the ring back out to show Will who whistles when he sees it.

"She'll love it, Alex," he says, and I grin at him, and he grins back, and then he goes back into work mode and his expression is once more the stoic nothing I have come to expect at work.

"Ok, one more time, just because I'm a good friend and I want you to be happy," Celia says on the way back to the car. "Are you absolutely sure Ros is the one? Are you certain there's no one better suited to being with you that you just might not have considered for whatever reason?"

"She's definitely the one and there is no one better suited to me," I say.

"But-" Celia starts.

I cut her off.

"That's enough Celia. You have checked in like a good

friend and I have answered your question. Now keep being a good friend and just be happy for me," I say.

"Got it," she says.

She doesn't have any other bitchy little comments to make as we head back to the office which I'm grateful for. All her assertions and questions have done is convince me I'm right about Ros, because when Celia was questioning me about how there could maybe be someone better suited to me, I couldn't imagine being with anyone other than Ros and that's all I need to know that I'm making the right choice in wanting to marry her. Now I just have to hope and pray that she feels the same way about me and says yes when I ask her.

When I ask her isn't really a concern for me – the sooner the better as far as I'm concerned, but the where of it is concerning me somewhat. I know people will say it doesn't matter and technically they are right, but I'd love to choose somewhere really special that Ros will love.

I start running scenarios through my head – a picnic on the beach, a moonlight stroll, in bed right after hot sex. The ideas are endless. I would love to have had the ring back when we watched the firework display at the theme park. There is something about fireworks that just makes everything more romantic somehow and I would have loved to propose to Ros during the display. That gives me an idea – maybe I can ask my aunt or my grandad to host another family barbecue and have our own little fireworks display during it. I'm not entirely sure of the logistics of it all yet, but I think it's my best idea so far and I will definitely be looking into it seriously.

"Are you ok?" Celia asks me as we walk back from the parking lot to the office building. "You've hardly spoken a word since we left the mall."

I can see no harm in telling her the truth.

"I was thinking about somewhere special for the actual proposal," I say.

"Oh, that's easy," Celia smiles. "There's no better romantic spot than the place you shared your first kiss."

I grimace, remembering that the first time we kissed was in my office and Celia groans.

"Oh God it was at work, wasn't it?" she says.

"It was outside of work hours, but yes, it was in the building," I say.

"Then ignore that idea. I don't think anyone wants to be proposed to at work. I'm sure there are worse places, but I can't think of any right now," she says.

"A morgue," I suggest, and we both laugh.

"I reckon that's about on a par with it," Celia says, and we laugh again.

We get in the elevator and go up to our floor. Celia stays at the reception desk, and I go on toward my office. Ros is at her desk, and she looks up and smiles at me as I approach her.

"Did you get everything taken care of?" she asks.

"Yes thanks," I say. "Any messages for me?"

"There's a couple. The details are on the system," she says.

"Thanks, Ros," I say and go into my office.

I know she's dying to ask where I've been and what I've been doing, and I'm just hoping she keeps stopping herself from doing so because I don't want to lie to her and I don't want to have to tell her to mind her own business, even in a nice way, but obviously I can't tell her the truth as it will kind of spoil the surprise proposal.

I sit down and get settled and then I start returning the calls Ros has listed on the system. There's nothing major for me to deal with and when I've finished, I decide to go and grab a can of soda from the kitchen. I get up and head across my office. I open the door and before it is fully open, I hear Celia's voice.

"Yes, we had a lovely lunch. You know, I'd forgotten how funny Alex can be," she says.

I'm instantly fuming. What the fuck is Celia playing at? She's obviously trying to make Ros think we had lunch together and cause shit between us. I open the door the rest of the way, but before I can step out of the office or speak, Celia spots me.

"Oh Alex, there you are. I was just on my way to discuss something with you," she says and heads for my office, ignoring the fact I was obviously on my way out. I decide to just let her bulldozer her way in because I want to have a serious word with her anyway after the little stunt she has just pulled back there. I back up into my office and Celia comes in and shuts the door behind her.

"You can't have any lunch today," she says. "At least not where Ros might see you. She asked about where we had been, and I told her we had lunch together."

"What? Why? Are you trying to piss her off or something?" I demand.

"Of course not. Why would you having some lunch with a friend piss her off? I was trying to give you an alibi that didn't involve shopping for rings," she says.

"Why did you feel the need to mention it at all?" I ask.

"Because one of the others told her we left together," Celia says. "Oh, it was innocent enough. Ros was looking for me and she just told her I was somewhere with you. She asked me if we'd been to see a client or something. I nearly said yes, but then I thought if she asks more questions, and I can't answer them, it's going to get messy."

I relax. Of course, Celia isn't trying to get between Ros and me or to make her angry at me. She's my friend and she's got my back, and she was just keeping my surprise quiet.

"Thanks Celia," I say. "Now, what can I do for you?"

"Nothing," she says. "I was just wanting to give you a

heads up in case Ros mentioned us having lunch together and you knew nothing about it."

I thank Celia again and then she leaves my office and I go to the kitchen for my can of soda as I originally planned to. I turn to leave the kitchen and Ros stands in the doorway. She smiles at me and comes over and kisses me quickly.

"You don't have to hide it from me if you want to have lunch with a friend, Alex. Even if the friend happens to be female," she says.

"I'm sorry," I say. "I should have told you."

"That's the thing," she says. "It's not a big deal. You don't have to specifically tell me, but you don't have to hide it from me either."

"You are the best girlfriend a guy could ask for, you know that?" I say, meaning it.

I pull her into my arms and kiss her again. She kisses me back, but not for as long as I would like her to.

"Relax. This is our private kitchen, remember," I say.

"I know, but it only takes someone seeing my desk empty and coming to look for me," she says.

I release her and I instantly miss the feeling of her body in my arms. She smiles at me again and leaves the room. I follow behind her with my soda and I can't help but watch her ass sway as she walks. I love that she's not the jealous type or if she is, she hides it really well, but I also know that once I've proposed to her, I will tell her what really happened today with Celia just in case she is a little bit more insecure than she'd like to let on about the whole thing, because while I do believe that she's not mad at me, the fact she instigated a kiss at work and not even in my office after her always being the careful one tells me she was just marking her territory in case I had forgotten about her or something.

CHAPTER
Twenty-Six
ALEX

"Come in," I call as a light tap comes on my office door. I'm expecting Will, but instead, Ros comes in.

"Oh," I say. "I thought you were Will."

"Sorry to disappoint you," Ros says.

"You could never disappoint me," I tell her.

She smiles at me and blows me a kiss.

"And that is the correct answer," she says. "Will went to the bathroom, I think. Do you have a minute before he gets back?"

I nod, and she comes walking over and sits down at my desk.

"Ok, so this is a bit of a strange one, but I just had a call from a potential new client. It's a medium sized firm and winning the contract will bring us a decent amount of business," Ros tells me.

"Ok," I say when she pauses. "What's strange about it?"

"I was just getting to that. She wants a meeting. Today. With me," Ros says. "I told her I would go because it seemed silly to lose a potential client by me saying no to a simple meeting."

"You do remember that you're my personal assistant, not an accountant or a sales representative, right?" I say with a raised eyebrow.

"Yes," Ros says. "And so does the potential client. I made it very clear to her and I made it clear that if she has questions, I might not be the best qualified person to answer them, but she insisted and she said if she decides she wants to go with us, she can ask those technical questions to someone else then."

"I don't mean to be rude, like no offense to you Ros, but it's beyond me why she wants a meeting with you," I say bluntly.

I wait for Ros's reaction, and she surprises me by nodding her head in agreement.

"I feel the same way and I did mention that to her several times, but she insisted. The company was recommended to her by Lance Donovan from Brannigan's and apparently, he mentioned me by name and spoke very highly of me, so she wants to meet with me," Ros tells me.

Another knock sounds on my office door before I can process what Ros has said.

"Mr. Popular today," she says with a smile.

"Tell me about it," I say, grimacing instead of smiling. Ros laughs. "Come in."

The door opens and Will appears in the gap.

"Oh, sorry, I didn't know you were in the middle of something," Will says.

He goes to close the door, but I stop him.

"No, don't go," I say. "It was me who asked to see you remember. Sit down, we won't be much longer and it's nothing you can't hear."

Will nods his head and comes into my office and quietly

pushes the door shut behind him. He doesn't sit down. Instead, he walks over to the window and stands looking out at the city with his back to Ros and me, giving us the only privacy he can in this situation.

"Right, where were we?" I say to Ros. "Yes, you were telling me about this woman who wants a meeting with you."

Ros nods her head.

"I said I would meet her at one," she says. I glance at my watch and see it's already twelve thirty. "But obviously if you want to take the meeting instead, feel free. Or I can call her back and cancel the whole thing altogether."

I think for a moment.

"No, let's just play it her way. I can't see any harm in you having a meeting with her. As long as you're comfortable with that?" I say and Ros nods her head. "Good. Do you want to take one of the accountants with you?"

"I'd rather not at this stage," Ros says. "I'd rather get to know her needs and then from there see who will be the best suited to her."

"OK, that's fine," I say. "What's the company called?"

I see Ros cringe a little and I raise an eyebrow.

"As stupid as it sounds, I forgot to ask. I just took her name and the address. She's Camilla Monroe, and the address is Unit Eight on the Mason Avenue Trading Estate," Ros says.

I think for a moment, but I can't place what company is there.

"Ok, off you go before you end up running late. Call me if you need to," I say.

"Thanks," Ros says, and she gets up.

"Go get her," I say and Ros grins.

"I will," she says.

She leaves the office and I turn my attention to Will.

"I just wanted to go over next month's itinerary with you so you know roughly where I will be and when, see if you need to change anything with your team," I say. "To be honest, it's a pretty standard month, nothing exciting happening."

Unless I find the opportunity to propose to Ros and she says yes of course. I don't say this though. I'm sure Will won't mind shifting a few things around if I do manage to fit the proposal in. He's always good like that.

Will nods and comes over to my desk. He looks over the itinerary I've done for him to show him where I will be on what days, and he nods his head.

"That's fine," he says. "Can I take this copy?"

I nod and Will takes it and leaves my office once more.

CHAPTER
Twenty-Seven
WILL

I take my position up again outside of Alex's office door. I don't know why, but I keep thinking about Ros going off to that meeting and the address she gave Alex. Something about it is nagging at me. Call it intuition, something that I have honed over the years because of my profession, but something about it just felt off to me when Alex and Ros were discussing it.

I know I shouldn't have been listening, but it's kind of hard not to when you're in a room with two other people and no background noise and they are talking to each other. It's part of the job that I hear stuff and that I'm supposed to then just forget about it or at the very least pretend that I have.

For example, that night we went on the business trip, of course I heard Alex and Ros fucking, but I would never have said as much. Or the times I've seen Celia being a complete bitch to Ros until Alex comes along and then she plays nice, but again, I pretend like I haven't noticed. I know Ros knows I've noticed, because the odd time I haven't been able to help it but to laugh at Ros's come backs, but I pretend like I didn't see or hear a thing if anyone asks and as much as I would like to tell Alex his friend is a fucking bitch when his back is turned, I don't, because it's not my place to say it. Unless Alex asks me something directly about her, or unless she begins to pose a danger to Alex's safety, I will store the information away in the 'things I didn't hear but I did hear them' box.

The address Ros gave Alex should very much be in that box, but whenever I try to put it away in there, it nags at me again and it won't let me forget it. In the end I decide to do a quick Google search on the address. Once I find out what company it is, I might be able to put an end to the nagging thoughts of the address and move on. It's probably a pizza place I've used or something and that's why it stood out to me because it's familiar without me knowing why.

I pull my cell phone out of my jacket pocket and open up my Google app. I quickly type the address in and hit search. No company name or anything comes up as the first result which is not what I was expecting. I scroll down a bit and scan the results, but there's nothing. I move onto the second page, something I rarely if ever do, and then I spot a company name I recognize; Tate's Cars.

Now I know why the address was familiar to me. A friend of mine worked for Tate's Cars and a few months ago, they had gone bust, and he had found himself out of a job which he had been telling me about, hence my recognition. But if they have gone bust, why on earth are they looking for an accountant?

The obvious answer is that a different company has taken over the building and knowing that should be enough for me, but it's not. Somehow, the more I get answers here the more my intuition tells me something is very wrong here. I need to double check everything before I act on it though. I don't think Alex will be too happy if I tell him my suspicions and we go over there only to find a perfectly respectable and thriving business there. And Ros will always think Alex didn't trust her to take the meeting and came to spy on her, regardless of what he tells her.

I dig further into Tate Cars and the building on the trading estate. I learn that the building is actually pretty big, and as well as using it as the dispatch office for the cars, it was also used to store the cars in the warehouse side of it. Other than that, I don't learn anything new about the building and I change my search terms and start again. This time, I do learn something, but it's not what I wanted to see.

The building still very much belongs to Tate Cars. They've been trying to sell it since they went into liquidation, but the trading estate itself is pretty run down and no one seems interested in buying the unit. It's just standing empty, falling into more disrepair and becoming less likely to sell by the minute.

Next, I google Camilla Monroe. There are thousands of hits, but most of them are just social media profiles of various people named Camilla Monroe. I think for a moment and then I add the words Mason Avenue Trading Estate. That will narrow it down a bit and it should bring up any business there associated with this woman. There are no results that make that match.

I have no idea who Camilla Monroe is, but I know she isn't running a business based in Unit Eight of Mason Avenue Trading Estate. Is Ros walking into some sort of trap? I stay calm but only because of years of training. It seems to me that Ros might be about to be taken hostage and used against Alex.

I turn around and open Alex's office door, not bothering to knock. He looks up as I walk in.

"I think Ros might be in danger," I say.

"How?" Alex asks, still looking at me.

"That address she gave you. Something about it was familiar and it was nagging at me, so I Googled it. The business that was based there went into liquidation a few months ago, but they still own the building. They can't sell it. That alone made me suspicious, and there is also no record of a Camilla Monroe having a business there. I don't want to worry you, but I think maybe someone is trying to lure Ros into a trap so they can take her and use her to get money from you," I say.

Alex jumps to his feet, and I hold my hands up to him to try and calm him down. I can see the panic on his face.

"Sit down," I say. "And try not to panic. I'm going to go over there now and take a look around. There's probably some innocent explanation for all of this."

"It sounds pretty fucking shady Will," Alex says.

I nod. I can't lie. It does sound shady.

"Then I will make sure Ros is ok and bring her back to you," I say.

Alex shakes his head.

"I'm coming with you," he says.

"No, you're not," I say. "This could be dangerous."

"I've never done this, and I have never wanted to have to, but we're wasting time arguing about it and this is too important for me to take a back seat on. I'm your boss and I'm telling you that I am going with you. It isn't open to debate. I accept the risks and if anything happens to me, it will be on my head not yours," Alex says.

He's right about us wasting time so I don't argue, I just turn and run toward the elevators with Alex in tow. As we ride down, I try one last time to talk Alex out of coming with me.

"As my boss, your life is my priority, Alex. Your being here for this might slow me down, because I will be focusing on worrying about where you are and if you're safe instead of worrying about Ros," I say.

"As your boss, your priority is whatever I tell you it needs to be, and right now, I want it to be Ros. Forget about me. I will make sure I don't get in your way. Just make sure she's alright. Please Will, I don't know what I would do without her, and I know I can't just sit here and let you go off without me. It would drive me crazy," Alex says.

I can hear from his voice that he really loves Ros and my resolve to jump in my car and speed off and leave him behind melts away. He's right. If he just sits about here, it will make him crazy.

"Ok," I say. "But once we get there, this is my operation, and I am the boss. If I say hold back, you hold back. If I tell you to do something, you do it without question because lives – yours, mine and Ros's – might just depend on it. Is that clear?"

"Perfectly," Alex says.

"And you agree to it?" I press him.

"Yes," he says.

I'm sure that in the moment, he does mean it, but I also know that depending on what we find when we get to the trading estate, all of that could change. I have no doubt that Alex won't hesitate to throw himself into danger to save Ros. I'm going to have to be extra vigilant here and make sure he doesn't get the chance to do anything heroic and stupid. That's my job, not his.

CHAPTER
Twenty-Eight
ALEX

I follow Will across the lobby and out of the office building to the parking lot. I don't argue when he goes for his car instead of mine. I don't care whose car we go in as long as we get there and get there quickly. I dive into the passenger seat as Will gets in the driver's seat and I barely have the door shut when he pulls away, his tires screeching.

I think that scares me more than anything. Not that I think he's going to crash the car and kill us both or anything. I think when he pulls away like that, it hits me how seriously he's taking this. It isn't just me overreacting. Will is the most level-headed person I know, and if he's reacting this way, then there's definitely a better than average chance that something is very wrong here.

I should have known myself when the so-called client wanted to meet with Ros alone. Why the hell would anyone wanting financial services want to meet up with a personal assistant from the finance company. Even with the personal recommendation from Lance Donovan, it would have only really made sense if the woman had demanded a meeting with me or one of the senior accountants and asked Ros to sit in.

The worst thing is, I knew it sounded weird and I let her go anyway. I mean don't get me wrong, I never imagined for a second she might have been in danger, or I never would have let her go, but I should have thought it through more, I should have done a search on the address like Will did. I should have gone with her. Something. Anything. I should have stopped her from going.

"Are you ok?" Will asks as he hurtles through the traffic, dodging in and out of lanes, trying to get through the roads as quickly as he can.

"No," I say honestly. "I should never have let her go to this stupid fake meeting. If anything happens to her…"

I trail off, not even wanting to think about anything happening to her.

"It's not your fault Alex. There was no reason for you to stop her from going. You didn't know the business there closed down and if you'd tried to stop her from going, she would have argued back and probably went anyway. You know what Ros is like," Will says.

I know he's trying to make me feel better, but I also know that he's not wrong about Ros. She wouldn't have let a little thing like my instructions stop her from doing something if she really thought it was the best thing to do, and I feel like she definitely thought her taking this meeting would be the best course of action and gain us a new client.

"Are we nearly there?" I ask Will, well aware that I sound like a whiny, impatient child.

"About halfway," Will says.

"Fuck," I say. "Can't you go any faster?"

"Sure I can if you want me to hit the car in front of us," Will says.

"Ok, point taken," I say.

"I'm not dragging my feet here Alex," Will says. "For what it's worth, Ros has grown on me too and I would hate to see anything bad happen to her."

That makes me feel better. I know Will is a good man and that he would try and save Ros anyway, but if he didn't much like her, I think he would worry more about keeping me safe than trying to reach her in time. This way, I know he really will do everything he can to get to her in time.

"We won't be too late, will we?" I ask. "I mean we didn't set off that much later than she did, and she won't have been speeding across the town like we are."

"I think, if traffic stays the same as it is now and the traffic conditions were similar for Ros, we'll be five minutes behind her tops," Will says.

On the one hand, five minutes isn't very long at all. But on the other hand, five minutes is a fucking eternity. I guess it depends on the context. If she's having a genuine meeting with someone representing a new company who has purchased this building and just haven't had the paperwork go through yet, five minutes is about right to have done basic greetings, offer refreshments and just be starting in on the important stuff. If she has been lured into some sort of a trap, five minutes is more than enough to have strung her up and maybe even killed her. God no. I can't think of that. I won't let myself even think of it as a possibility.

I look out of the window, trying to mentally make the cars in front of us move out of the fucking way. It doesn't work obviously but it's better than being trapped inside of my own horrible thoughts right now. I know I need to think positive, but I can't, because the thought of convincing myself everything is ok and then finding out something has happened to Ros is just too much. It would break me completely and if anything has happened to her, I need my wits about me to make whoever hurt her pay. It's better that I just don't think of the end game here at all.

"We're almost there," Will says and I turn my attention back to him and the GPS system on his dashboard.

We have less than a minute of driving time to go as Will pulls off the main street and drives down a smaller, secondary street whose sign tells me it's Mason Avenue. For once, something goes right for us, and Mason Avenue is blessedly empty. Will really puts his foot down, and the minute's time reduces to twenty seconds. I see a sign welcoming us to the Mason Avenue Trading Estate as we whip around the corner, practically on two wheels.

Will slows down for a brief second and then speeds up again and heads left. I realize he was looking at the directory board to find Unit Eight and I trust that he did find it before he sped up again.

"When we get out of the car, stay behind me," Will says. "I mean it Alex."

"I will," I say.

I have no intention in doing so unless he's fast enough that I have no choice, but I'm not going to waste another second of my time arguing with him. We wasted enough time back at the office discussing whether or not this place seemed dodgy before we decided that it did.

The car skids to a halt and Will cuts the engine. We're both out of the car and running toward the building that has a large white square above the door with a big red number eight printed on it.

My stomach rolls with nausea when I spot Ros's car parked on the next curb. She must have overshot slightly and decided just to stay there. There are other cars parked there too, but I figure they belong to people in the other unit. Although one could belong to Camilla Monroe or whoever the hell Ros is really meeting here.

Will reaches the door to the building one step ahead of me and he tests the door handle. The door opens – hopefully a good sign because surely it means that someone is here - and he pushes it slowly, putting his finger to his lips telling me to be quiet so that he can listen. I want to shove him aside and just get in there, but I know he's doing the right thing, gathering any intel available to us. If Ros is in danger, us busting in and startling her tormenter could spell the end for her.

After a second, Will slips inside of the building and beckons at me to follow him. I do so and he gently closes the door behind us. We're in a large space, the walls whitewashed and the floor swept concrete. A large metal shelving unit clings to the wall opposite us. There are no windows, and I can't see any other external doors and the place is lit by strip lights set in the ceiling.

CHAPTER
Twenty-Nine
ALEX

There's no sign of anyone being here. The small office part of the unit is walled off. It has a small internal window, but the blinds are closed, and I can't see in. It's the only place Ros and Camilla can be though if they are still here at all. I don't want to get my hopes up too much, but I feel slightly better than I did a moment ago before we came into the building. Surely if someone wanted to hold Ros against her will and hurt her, they would just do it out here. Why bother doing it in the office?

I'm starting to have a feeling that Will and I are going to come out of this looking mighty stupid, and once we're back at the office, we will be the butt of Ros's jokes for a while, but that's a very small price to pay for her to just be safe. She can tease me for the rest of my life about it if she wants to, as long as she's by my side, I don't care.

Will moves toward the wall furthest from the window in the little office area and he beckons for me to follow him, so I do. Through a series of points, gestures, and the odd mouthed word, Will tells me that the office door is open a crack, so we need to be silent in our approach, and that we are going to come to the office from the right, hugging the wall all the way to make sure both us and our shadows stay out of sight. We will listen and determine our next course of action once we're close enough to hear what, if anything, is happening in the office.

We creep along the wall, moving slower than I would like us to, but needing to so that we can be sure our approach is silent. I know what Will's logic behind the slow and silent method is, although he didn't say so, probably trying to spare me the worry. If someone does have Ros in there and it's someone who doesn't care about her life, there's nothing to stop them killing her if we come in loudly enough that they know we're coming. It's frustrating moving so slowly when the office is almost in touching distance, but I understand the need for it. It's better than Ros ending up getting hurt or worse.

We are a couple of feet from the open door when Will holds his hand up and we stop and listen. At first, I don't hear anything, but then a woman speaks.

"Why are you doing this?" she says.

It's Ros's voice and I feel such a mixture of emotions at the sound of it. Relief because she's alive. Fear because she sounds scared, and I still don't know what's happening to her or who has her here. Frustration because at the sound of Ros's voice, Will instantly puts his arm out to stop me from moving and urgently puts his fingers to his lips gesturing for me to remain silent. Again, I get it. He wants to assess the situation and make sure going in won't put Ros in danger, but I just want to bust in there and grab Ros and get her out of here.

"Did somebody get their gag off? Tut tut. Because you were a good little girlie and didn't scream, I won't damage that pretty little face of yours. Yet," another female voice replies. She speaks as though speaking to a baby, her voice high and sing song in its tone.

Call me old fashioned, but I'm shocked to hear the other voice is also a female voice. I guess in my mind, if Ros was being held captive, it was by three or four men dressed all in black with masks over their faces. It being a woman doing this never even occurred to me. Judging by the lack of response to the woman's words, I can only assume she is working alone, hence why she had to lure Ros out here instead of just ambushing her I suppose.

There is a rustling sound and then a muffled umm sound. From what I put together from the sounds the woman has put the gag back on Ros.

"You want to know why I'm doing this?" the woman says.

This time, her voice is normal, the baby voice gone, and Will and I exchange confused glances. The voice is Celia's voice, but it can't be Celia here doing this surely. If it hadn't been for the look on Will's face reflecting exactly how I felt when I heard the voice, I would have assumed I was mistaken, but for us both to think the same thing and both be wrong is a bit of a stretch of the imagination.

I start to edge forward and for a moment, Will lets me, but when I draw up level with him, he puts his hand on my arm to get my attention. He pulls on his ear lobe and I get this message – listen and see what's going on first.

For all I know Ros is gagged, I also know she's alive and judging from the way she spoke before she was regagged, she doesn't sound like she's hurt. I don't like it, but I can follow Will's instructions for a moment longer while we listen and maybe find out what the hell is going on here.

"I'll tell you. Why not? You might as well know why you're going to have to die," Celia says.

My insides go cold at her words, and even more so at the calm way she delivers them. She makes the threat of death sound casual, like she's just chatting to someone about something that they both know is going to happen and isn't that important in the big scheme of things.

I curse myself inside. How many times has Ros told me Celia hates her and I've said that's not true. How many times has Ros told me she's different when the two of them are alone together and I've told her she's paranoid. How many times has Ros told me that Celia has a nasty streak, and I've told her it's just Celia's humor and she needs to get to know her. I guess Ros was right all along. Celia really does hate her; she really is different when it's just the two of them alone together (or so she thinks) and she definitely has a major nasty streak.

Could I have prevented this if I had taken Ros's complaints about Celia more seriously? Honestly, probably not. Not liking a coworker isn't a sackable offense so she wouldn't have been let go, and it's not like even Ros thought she was dangerous, so chances are, nothing would have been done differently and we still would have been here. That doesn't stop me from feeling bad about this whole thing though. I should have taken Ros at her word instead of trying to minimize her feelings.

If she gets out of this alive (please God, she has to get out of this alive), then I will never, ever doubt her word again. I will never assume she's being paranoid or that she doesn't know someone well enough to know when they are joking and when they are serious.

"You took my job," Celia says. "And you can give me all that bullshit about it being your job first, but ultimately, I was promised the job before we even moved companies, therefore in my eyes, that was my job."

There is a certain logic to her words if you ignore the fact that she was also told that the assistant role was off the table before we moved companies.

"I know what you're thinking," Celia says. "You're

thinking I'm a total psycho doing this over a job. Well, if that's all this was about, you'd be right. But it's more than just that. See, once I got over the fact I'd been shafted with regards to the job, I also realized I'm basically coasting along now, answering calls and doing a bit of filing here and there, and I'm getting the same wages as when I was working late every night, constantly firefighting and never still. I made my peace with it."

"If things had stopped there, I'd have kept disliking you and you'd have kept disliking me and we would have gotten on with our lives. Or who knows, maybe we even would have grown to like each other. Dare I say it? Maybe we could even have become friends. Gross, right? But taking my job wasn't enough for you, was it? No. You had to take it all. Everything I wanted, everything I worked for, you came in and took away from me. Do you know what it feels like to lose everything? Do you?"

Her voice is getting shrill and she's shouting, and I'm feeling more and more on edge about holding back, but Will fixes me with a look, and I remind myself he's the expert here. He knows what he's doing, and I have to trust him to know when the right moment to make our move is coming up.

"No, of course you don't. Everything has always come easily for you hasn't it, Ros? Well, I'm here to show you what happens when you fuck with the wrong people. Or fuck the wrong person as the case may be. See I learned to live with you taking my job, but then you muscled in on Alex and started trying to take my one true love. And of course, Alex fell for your charms. Well, I can't let that happen. Alex is mine and I intend to keep it that way.

"I backed off at first because I knew Alex didn't particularly like you. And then you two got closer and I figured it was just a bit of chemistry and that anything between you two would fizzle out. But it didn't. Hell, even sending him evidence of you almost killing an ex didn't split you two up, did it? And so, it became time to take things into my own hands. So here we are."

"Here's how it will go down. At first, you'll be missing, and Alex will be out of his mind with worry, and good old Celia will be there for him, searching for you, reassuring him that it's not his fault, hugging him when he needs it. And if the search stays too cold, I'll call a tip in, and we'll find your body. Alex will be devastated, and I will help him through his grief, and one day, he will start to feel better, and he will see who was there for him all along, and he will finally see that we'll be good together and he will fall in love with me, and we will live a long and happy life together without you getting in the way."

CHAPTER
Thirty
ALEX

Ros makes a muffled sound through the gag. I love that she's not letting Celia feel like she's winning, even if she is. The sound Ros makes isn't a scared little whimper like I'm sure Celia wanted. Instead, it's a groan of rebellion, a sound that tells me that Ros isn't going down without a fight. I know being gagged will be driving her crazy because she can't say anything back to Celia and her wild ideas. I'm sure Ros wants to say something along the lines of *'all of the grief in the world wouldn't make him fall in love with you'*. At least I hope that's the kind of thing she would want to say, because it's certainly true.

In the past, up until like ten minutes ago when we got here and realized who has Ros, I would have said Celia was a friend of mine. A good friend even. But that's all it was. I've never been attracted to her, and I never will. In theory, I get that she's pretty and most men would kill for her, but she's just not my type, and with or without Ros in the picture that won't change.

Will is edging forward again and I join him. He doesn't bother telling me to remain silent. He doesn't need to. One wrong word from either of us and Ros could be dead before we can grab Celia if Celia has a gun or any sort of weapon ready.

We get close enough finally that I can see inside of the office. There isn't much to see – bare, cream walls, a bare floor and one chair in the middle of it. I assume Celia brought the chair herself, because it's literally the only thing in here and the one thing Celia seems to have needed. Ros is on the chair and my heart just about breaks at the sight of her like this. Her hands are pulled behind her back, held together with lashings of packing tape. Her ankles are bound together in a similar fashion. A scarf is tied around her head, being used as a gag. The only good thing I can take from the situation is that she doesn't look to be hurt except for a cut on the right side of her forehead, which I can only assume came from Celia hitting her with something to knock her unconscious so she could secure her to the chair. Bitch. I swear I will make her pay for this.

Celia is standing a few feet away from Ros. Ros glares at her and again, I'm glad to see her doing that instead of crying and begging for Celia to free her. I know how much it will piss Celia off that Ros doesn't seem to be afraid of her.

"Goodbye Ros," Celia says, and she moves her hand to her back. It comes back with a gun in it. A gun which she points at Ros.

I've seen enough, and I don't care what Will says about me staying out of danger. Celia is about to kill the love of my life and there is no way in hell I'm just going to stand here and let that happen.

Will is starting to move, but I'm faster, and I burst into the room. Both Celia and Ros turn their heads in my direction and both of them stare at me in shock. Everything seems to go in slow motion, although I'm sure in reality this is all over in a second or two.

Celia's thumb moves and flicks the safety off the gun. Even though she is looking at me, the gun is still trained on Ros.

"Celia, stop. Put the gun down," I say.

Celia shakes her head, but she doesn't shoot Ros, and I take that to mean there's still a small chance of talking her down if I can find the right words. Will is standing beside me now and I can feel he is silently fuming with me for ignoring his instructions, but he keeps quiet, his eyes darting around, assessing the room and what can be done to end this situation with everyone alive and no one hurt.

"I heard what you said Cee. About loving me," I say.

"And?" she demands.

I could tell her I love her too, make her think there's a chance for us if she puts the gun down, but I know I'm not a good enough actor to pull that off. Even Celia confirms it for me with her next sentence.

"And don't think I'm stupid enough to fall for the whole I love you too, let's be together shit, because I know you're going to try it and I know it's going to be a trap to get the gun away from me," she says.

"I don't think you're stupid for a second," I say. "Hence why I wasn't going to even bother trying that. Here's what I will say, and I mean it one hundred percent. I'm sorry. I'm sorry I didn't notice your feelings for me went beyond friendship, and I'm so sorry I hurt you, even though that was never my intention."

"If you had known, would it have been different?" she says.

Again, I don't think lying to her is the right move.

"Honestly, I don't think it would have been different romantically," I say. "But I certainly would have been more aware of your feelings and made sure you weren't having my relationship with Ros put in your face."

"And if you'd never met Ros. What about then? Would there have been a chance for us?" Celia says.

I can see that this time she needs me to lie to her. She's going to keep asking questions about scenario after scenario until she finds one where we could have been together, and I feel like the longer it takes for her to be offered one, the more danger Ros's life is going to be in.

"I can't say for sure Cee, because I don't think anyone knows anything like that for sure. But yeah, maybe there would have been," I say.

Celia's face lights up and then she looks down at the gun and looks back at Ros and I realize in that moment that I have made a horrible mistake.

"So, if she's out of the picture, then maybe one day, you will be mine," she says.

I'm already running toward her, hoping I can reach her and wrestle the gun away from her, when she pulls the trigger. The noise is almost deafening in the small space, but it doesn't stop me from acting. I jump into the air as Celia fires, throwing myself in front of Ros, because if no one gets between her and that bullet, it's going to kill her.

I feel a pain in my stomach like I've been punched, and all of the wind goes out of me. The punched area begins to burn, and I feel warm blood running over my skin. I hit the floor hard and lay there, stunned. I try to breathe, but I can't. It feels as though my throat and the tubes in my chest have all tightened up too much to breathe. The agony in my stomach is making me feel sick and dizzy and the lack of oxygen isn't helping.

I'm vaguely aware of the others in the room. As the bullet hit me, because I know that's what that punching sensation was, Celia screamed out a long, drawn-out no. Ros did the best attempt at a scream that she could bearing in mind she's gagged. Will cursed, and I don't know if he was cursing Celia for shooting me or cursing me for not letting him be the one to take the bullet. I wasn't playing hero. I don't care who took the bullet as long as it wasn't Ros. I just knew I had to stop her from being shot, and if I die doing it, then that's ok, because my life wouldn't have been worth living without her in it anyway.

I know I'm losing blood rapidly, and I try to press my hands to my wound, but they won't move. It's like they weigh a thousand pounds each. I finally manage to breathe though so that's a bonus even though it hurts like a bastard because the pain is better than that claustrophobic, dying of suffocation feeling. I take another deep breath and then the pain in my stomach becomes too much and it overwhelms me, and everything goes black.

My last thought is a silent prayer to Ros, telling her that I love her and asking her to forgive me.

CHAPTER
Thirty-One
WILL

As we shuffle forward and bring the office into view, I want Alex behind me, but he's beside me instead. I don't need to tell him to keep silent, he knows that already, but I need to tell him to back off a bit. I stop myself though because I feel like if I give him that signal, the anger and fear that I can feel coming off him in waves are going to stop him from thinking rationally and he might call out and give away our position.

I scan the room. It doesn't take long. There's Ros secured to a chair and Celia standing opposite her, and that's it. Other than that, the room is empty. It's good because it gives me a clear line of sight to both Ros and Celia, but it's also bad because there's nothing to hide behind as I advance on Celia. I'm going to have to get the timing just right to make a grab for her.

Celia finishes her speech to Ros about why she's doing this to her. She really is off the charts crazy but that's someone else's problem. My problem is getting Alex and Ros away from her unhurt.

Celia reaches behind herself with one hand, and I know

she's going for a gun. I start to move, but somehow, Alex is ahead of me, and he bursts into the room, making no attempt to be quiet about it, although I think we are far beyond the point where that would have been useful anyway.

Celia turns her head toward Alex. Her face shows her shock at seeing him there. Ros looks at Alex too despite having a gun trained on her. That moment where all of the attention is on Alex works for me and I ease into the room and start to edge around Alex.

Celia is still looking at Alex as she takes the safety off the gun. The click sound it makes echoes hollowly through the room and I tense, waiting for the shot. I need to see if she's going to stick with shooting Ros or move her gun barrel toward Alex at the last minute before I act. Instead of the shot I'm waiting for, the only sound to come is Alex speaking.

"Celia, stop. Put the gun down," he says. He lifts his hands slightly in surrender and keeps his voice calm and soothing. That's good. If Celia hears panic in his voice, it might cause her to panic and that could be lethal at this point.

Celia shakes her head, and keeps the gun trained on Ros, but she doesn't shoot, and she seems interested in what Alex might have to say. While Celia is focused on Alex, I look around for something, anything, that can help end this stand-off, but there's nothing and I silently fume at Alex for putting himself in danger like this. He should have let me handle it. I should have insisted he stay at the office.

"I heard what you said Cee. About loving me," I hear Alex say and I turn my focus to the situation at hand. I can be mad at Alex later.

"And?" Celia says, clearly wanting to hear that Alex loves her too. I'm pretty sure that's not going to happen, because he loves Ros, and he won't deny that with Ros sitting right there.

"And don't think I'm stupid enough to fall for the whole I love you too, let's be together shit, because I know you're going to try it and I know it's going to be a trap to get the gun away from me," Celia adds.

I don't think you're stupid for a second," Alex tells her, keeping his voice at that calm tone that seems to be working a little bit. "Hence why I wasn't going to even bother trying that. Here's what I will say, and I mean it one hundred percent. I'm sorry. I'm sorry I didn't notice your feelings for me went beyond friendship, and I'm so sorry I hurt you, even though that was never my intention."

"If you had known, would it have been different?" Celia asks.

I wish we had the chance to discuss what answers Alex should give Celia to these questions, because one wrong word could trigger her and cause her to kill Ros, but Alex seems to be handling it well and for now, I think the safest option for everyone is to let this play out and see if he can persuade her to stop this before it goes any further.

"Honestly, I don't think it would have been different romantically," Alex replies. I don't know if that's a good idea, but Alex is a terrible liar so maybe it's for the best that he doesn't try to lie to Celia. But I don't think that's the answer she wanted to hear all the same. "But I certainly would have been more aware of your feelings and made sure you weren't having my relationship with Ros put in your face."

"And if you'd never met Ros. What about then? Would there have been a chance for us?" Celia says.

He needs to lie here and do it well. Come on Alex, I think, silently rooting for him to end this without any blood being spilled.

"I can't say for sure Cee, because I don't think anyone knows anything like that for sure. But yeah, maybe there would have been," he says.

Celia's face lights up and I thank God Alex said the right thing. The feeling is extremely short lived though. Celia finally looks away from Alex. She looks down at the gun in her hand and steadies it.

"So, if she's out of the picture, then maybe one day, you will be mine," she says.

The second she speaks; I know she's done talking and is about to shoot Ros with the aim of killing her. I start to move, but Alex is already running toward Celia. Fuck. He knows better than this.

I look from Alex to Celia just in time to see Celia's hand tense up as she pulls the trigger. The sound of the blast in such close quarters makes my ears ring, but that's the least of my worries right now. As Celia pulled the trigger, Alex jumped into the air, throwing himself in the path of the bullet so it hits him instead of Ros.

The bullet hits him in the stomach, just below his belly button and he slams down on the ground in a shower of bloody droplets.

"Fuck," I yell.

At the same time, Ros makes a garbled sound through her gag which is either a scream, or her calling Alex's name or maybe both.

"Nooooo," Celia yells as it hits her what she has done.

I stand on the spot, motionless for a moment. For once, I find myself torn, unsure of what course of action to take next. Do I go to Alex and try to save his life? He is laying in a spreading pool of blood, and he is either dead already or unconscious. If I go to him, Celia gets away, and if he's dead then she gets away for nothing. So, do I go after Celia? And if Alex isn't dead, he is bound to be if I don't go to him now and try to stop the bleeding. What do I do? Who do I choose?

I can hear Ros sobbing through the gag, and I think that sound makes my choice for me as much as anything else. I run to Alex and throw myself on my knees on the ground beside him. Celia sees her chance now that the doorway is clear, and she runs through it. Every instinct in me says to chase the bitch and make sure she pays for this, but I can't leave Alex. Not now that I can see he is breathing.

His chest is rising and falling feebly, and his skin is an ashy gray color, but he's alive and it's my job to keep him that way. I pull my t-shirt over my head and roll it into a ball, and I press it against the wound in Alex's stomach. I will just have to pray it's only a surface wound and it hasn't damaged any major organs.

Once I have the t-shirt in place, I hold it firmly with one hand, and with the other hand, I fumble in my jeans pocket for my cell phone. My hands are slippery with blood, and it falls to the floor.

"Fuck," I say again.

I feel like fuck is the only word left in my vocabulary that sums up what is happening here. I wipe my hand down the leg of my jeans and try again with my cell phone. I manage to keep a hold on it this time and unlock the keypad. I bring the cell phone up to my face and use my nose to hit the nine and then the one twice, and then the call symbol. I bring the cell phone to my ear, still holding onto Alex's wound.

"Nine one one, what's your emergency," the dispatcher says in my ear.

"I need an ambulance and the police to Unit Eight, Mason Avenue Trading Estate, Mason Avenue," I say. "I have a male, thirty-five, with a gunshot wound. He's rapidly losing blood. The shooter has made a run for it. She's female, thin, her hair is a bright red bob, and she is wearing a pair of black tailored trousers, high heels, and a peach-colored silk blouse. Please hurry, I need to hang up now."

"I have dispatched an ambulance and a police unit. Please stay on the line sir," the dispatcher says.

"I can't," I say. "As I said, the victim is losing a lot of blood and I need both hands to stem the bleeding."

I don't wait to hear her argument for me staying on the line, I just throw my cell phone aside. So, I suppose technically, I have stayed on the line as I didn't actually end the call.

"Come on Alex, wake up," I whisper to Alex.

He doesn't and his lips are going a light blue color which I don't think is a good sign. I press on his wound with both hands and the blood flow does seem to be slowing down now. If the ambulance gets here quickly enough, I think there might be hope for Alex yet.

CHAPTER
Thirty-Two
WILL

I've been in my own little bubble since the gunshot went off, but now I realize I can hear Ros crying and I glance over at her. She is sitting with her head down, sobbing. I instantly feel awful for leaving her in that state, but stopping Alex from bleeding out is more urgent and I know if I so much as tried to go and free Ros while Alex is bleeding out, she would be the first one to tell me to get back to him. That doesn't mean I can't reassure her a little bit though.

"Ros," I say. "Ros, listen to me. He's breathing."

She finally looks up and although tears run down her face, I see a light in her eyes at the words.

"He's going to be ok," I say, praying that's not a lie. "The ambulance is on its way."

It feels like forever before I hear a siren in the distance, but really is probably not more than three or four minutes. The siren gets closer and closer until it is right on top of us and then it cuts out and a few seconds later, the main door of the unit opens.

"Hello? Anyone here? Paramedics," a voice shouts.

"In here. Hurry," I call back.

I hear feet running toward the office and then two paramedics burst in. One gets on the ground opposite me, and the other one comes down beside me.

"We've got this," he says, taking over pressing on my t-shirt.

I get to my feet and go over to Ros while the paramedics work on stabilizing Alex. I hear more sirens and I figure this must be the police coming too. By the time two officers arrive in the small office, I've taken Ros's gag off, and torn the tape from her wrists and ankles. She is sobbing in my arms when the officers appear.

"I'm Officer Collier. This is my partner, Officer Davis," the male officer says, nodding to his female partner. "Was it you who made the nine one one call sir?"

I nod and quickly tell him what happened. He nods his head and then gets on his radio putting out a call for everyone to be on the watch for Celia. He gives a good description of her and then he comes back to us.

"I'll need you two to come down to the station and make an official statement," he says.

"No," Ros says. It's the first thing I've heard her say with any sort of force since I ungagged her. "I'm going to the hospital with Alex."

The officers look at me as though I'm going to somehow magically convince Ros to do as they say. Not only am I not even going to try, but I'm going to back her up.

"The statements can wait surely. You have the suspect's description and it's not like you've even caught her yet," I say.

The two officers exchange looks and nod to each other. Officer Collier turns his attention back to us.

"Ok. But we will need official statements. How about you guys drop by the station in the morning?" he says.

I nod.

"We'll be there," I say, speaking for us both.

Ros is watching the paramedics working on Alex and her face has gone deathly white and she looks like she's in a trance.

"This one looks like she might be going into shock," Officer Davis says, nodding at Ros.

"Don't worry, I'll keep my eye on her. We'll be following the ambulance to the hospital in my car and she's in the right place if she needs medical attention," I say.

Officer Davis doesn't look like she's completely happy to let it go, but in the end, she shrugs one of her shoulders and nods her head. There's not much else she can do. She knows as well as I do that calling an ambulance for a non-emergency will take forever. It will be quicker to drive myself and she knows Ros isn't going to want to go anywhere but the hospital so it's not like she's going to be at risk. Besides, she's done her duty by warning me and I have taken responsibility for the problem so she's off the hook.

The officers talk to one of the paramedics for a moment, likely passing on the information about Ros, because after a second, he comes over and wraps a blanket around her shoulders while his colleague walks out of the office with the police officers. The paramedic comes back alone with a gurney and between the two paramedics, they get Alex onto the gurney and then they start to wheel him away. We follow and then I remember my discarded cell phone and go and grab it. The dispatcher has long since ended the call, so I put the cell phone away in my pocket. I hurry to catch up with Ros who is following the gurney on unsteady looking legs. She takes my offered arm when I reach them, and we watch as the paramedics then open the doors at the back of the ambulance and lift the gurney into it. One of the paramedics climbs into the back of the ambulance, pulling the gurney into the back, securing it and then the other one slams the doors.

"We'll be right behind you," I say, and he nods his head and then he jogs around to the driver's side of the ambulance. The engine fires up, the siren starts, and the ambulance pulls away. I lead Ros to my car and open the door for her. She gets in and I close the door and rush around to the driver's side. I start the car up and hurry after the ambulance, all the while praying that Alex will be ok.

CHAPTER
Thirty-Three

ROS

I sit in the passenger seat beside Will as he drives toward the hospital, and I find myself wondering exactly how the hell this all happened. Less than two hours ago, I was sitting at my desk at work, happy and normal and looking forward to a date night with Alex. Now my head hurts, and Alex might die. Oh my God, Alex might die. What the fuck? It doesn't feel real, but I know it is, and if I start to doubt it, I only need to poke the wound on my forehead and the stab of pain I feel from it brings me back to reality.

Over these last two hours, I've run the gauntlet of emotions, peaking and plunging more than I thought was ever possible, especially in so short a space of time. I remember getting the phone call from Celia, who at the time was calling herself Camilla Monroe and her asking me to have a meeting with her. I remember being so proud because a new client wanted to talk to me, and I might be the one to bring in the new business for the company. I was a fucking idiot though. There was no client, just pain, humiliation and possible death. Celia disguised her voice, but I still should have known there was something off, even if I didn't click it was her. I guess I just figured because she mentioned one of our clients and it was one who I genuinely have a fair bit of input with, that it was real, and I just believed it. Probably mostly because I wanted to believe it.

I drove out to the address both happy and nervous, but the kind of nervous that comes from wanting to do a good job, not from actually being afraid. Even when I reached the unit and it looked deserted it didn't dampen my spirits. If anything, it made sense because a new company was moving in, and they would want to renovate the place to their specifications first.

I suppose I should have thought it was odd when I called out to announce my arrival at the already open door, and a voice shouted back for me to go to the office. In hindsight, I guess it wasn't that weird the door was open if someone was really looking out for me. But the fact they didn't even stick their head around the door when I arrived should have been a red flag. But no. At that point, I was still thinking about what I was going to say and do to make a good impression. The next half an hour or, however long it took, is ingrained in my memory and as I look out of the window of Will's car, it's not the passing scenery I see, but instead, the time I spent as Celia's prisoner plays out before me like a movie that I'm watching myself star in.

I stepped into the office, and it was empty except for a single chair. I didn't see anyone who the voice could have belonged to, and I turned my head slightly, but before I could get a look at the person who was standing flush against the wall there, they hit me in the head with something damned hard, and I saw stars and then everything went black.

I woke up with my wrists and ankles restrained sitting in the one chair. I was gagged and I was alone. That's when my joy and nerves vanished, replaced by absolute terror and mild confusion. Like I wanted to know what the fuck had happened, but I was more concerned with why I was here and what was going to happen to me next. It was obvious at that point that I was in serious trouble, and I figured I was on my own. Only Alex and maybe Will knew where I was, but there was no reason for them to come looking for me while I was in a meeting with a client. It could be two or three hours before Alex even thought it was strange how long I'd been gone. And even then, he wouldn't assume I was in danger.

When I realized my captor was Celia, it did nothing to calm me down. In fact, I think if anything, my terror went up a notch. I was being held captive by someone who I knew didn't like me and who had now proved herself to be one hundred percent a raging psycho. I tried to ask her what she wanted from me, but I was gagged and all I could produce was a mumbling sound.

Celia told me she was going to move her car and I should just sit here and wait for her. I remember her laughing when she said it because it wasn't like I had a choice about sitting tight and waiting for her.

Yeah, great joke. The fucker should be on stage.

When she was gone, I tried to pry my hands apart, but I had no luck. I did manage to spit the gag out, but by then, I could hear Celia was back in the main area of the unit. I figured that if I screamed, there was a chance I wouldn't be heard by anyone from the nearby units. They were all detached and had a decent amount of space around them which would mean I would only stand a chance of being heard if one of the other units happened to have their door or windows open. And even then, they would likely assume it was just someone messing around, or they might decide that they didn't want to get involved and just pretend they hadn't heard anything. Even if they came to look, Celia could do anything to me by the time they got here. I would bide my time before giving Celia another reason to go for me.

I listen as Celia walks across the main unit area and then she slips back into the office. She glances at me, but she doesn't seem to notice the gag has come loose. I suppose it's because it's still technically on my face, just now the part that was in my mouth earlier is now on my chin.

She paces for a bit and her pacing gives off a nervous energy that makes me feel worse than I already do. I decide to try and get her talking. If nothing else, she might stay still instead of knocking me seasick with her pacing. I ask the obvious question first.

"Why are you doing this?" I ask.

Celia does stop pacing so there's that. She grins at me and then she shakes her head and starts to talk to me in a baby voice that sets my nerves on edge.

"Did somebody get their gag off? Tut tut. Because you were a good little girlie and didn't scream, I won't damage that pretty little face of yours. Yet," she says.

I don't get a second chance to ask anything else or to scream. Celia closes the gap between us and drags the gag back into my mouth and then resecures it tighter around my head. Fuck. That wasn't part of my plan. Not that I really had a plan in the first place, but if I did have one, I know this wouldn't have been a part of it.

"You want to know why I'm doing this?" Celia says walking back in front of me now that my gag is tightened. She stops a couple of feet away from me. I decide that yes, if I'm going to die here at her hand, I do at least want to know why. It has to be about more than her disliking me surely. "I'll tell you. Why not? You might as well know why you're going to have to die."

For all I kind of figured me dying was her end game, hearing her confirm it out loud is both shocking and strangely liberating. I don't have to keep second guessing why I'm here. Now I know. I feel like hearing her say that should make me more afraid, but it actually takes the edge off my fear – I guess it's true that most of our fear comes from the unknown.

"You took my job," Celia says. "And you can give me all that bullshit about it being your job first, but ultimately, I was promised the job before we even moved companies, therefore in my eyes, that was my job."

My eyes widen at her confession. I was going to try and keep my face neutral in case my reaction pissed her off, but when I heard this is all over a job, I couldn't help but show my shock.

"I know what you're thinking," Celia says. "You're thinking I'm a total psycho doing this over a job."

Yes. Yes, I am, I think to myself. I am sensible enough not to nod my agreement at that though. I just keep watching her and wait for her to go on.

"Well, if that's all this was about, you'd be right. But it's more than just that. See, once I got over the fact I'd been shafted with regards to the job, I also realized I'm basically coasting along now, answering calls and doing a bit of filing here and there, and I'm getting the same wages as when I was working late every night, constantly firefighting and never still. I made my peace with it.

"If things had stopped there, I'd have kept disliking you and you'd have kept disliking me and we would have gotten on with our lives. Or who knows, maybe we even would have grown to like each other. Dare I say it? Maybe we could even have become friends. Gross, right? But taking my job wasn't enough for you, was it? No. You had to take it all. Everything I wanted, everything I worked for, you came in and took it all away from me. Do you know what it feels like to lose everything? Do you?"

She pauses like she's waiting for an answer from me. She sounds like she's starting to come unhinged, and I'm afraid any answer I choose will be wrong, but I have to do something or being ignored might set her off. I nod, because after my time with Danny, I feel like I do know what it feels like to lose everything. Celia rolls her eyes and then carries on like I gave her the answer she wanted, the answer that makes me the villain in her eyes.

"No, of course you don't. Everything has always come easily for you hasn't it, Ros? Well, I'm here to show you what happens when you fuck with the wrong people. Or fuck the wrong person as the case may be. See I learned to live with you taking my job, but then you muscled in on Alex and started trying to take my one true love. And of course, Alex fell for your charms. Well, I can't let that happen. Alex is mine and I intend to keep it that way."

"I backed off at first because I knew Alex didn't particularly like you. And then you two got closer and I figured it was just a bit of chemistry and that anything between you two would fizzle out. But it didn't. Hell, even sending him evidence of you almost killing an ex didn't split you two up, did it? And so, it became time to take things into my own hands. So here we are."

"Here's how it will go down. At first, you'll be missing, and Alex will be out of his mind with worry, and good old Celia will be there for him, searching for you, reassuring him that it's not his fault, hugging him when he needs it. And if the search stays too cold, I'll call a tip in, and we'll find your body. Alex will be devastated, and I will help him through his grief, and one day, he will start to feel better, and he will see who was there for him all along, and he will finally see that we'll be good together and he will fall in love with me, and we will live a long and happy life together without you getting in the way."

I think if I wasn't gagged, I would have laughed at Celia's assumption that Alex would fall for her if she killed me. If Alex was going to fall for Celia, he would have done it already. As she keeps reminding me, she was his assistant for long enough before I came along. Instead of laughing, I make a groaning sound, one that I think is neutral enough for Celia to interpret it however she wants to.

I really need to figure out a way out of here, but I keep trying and trying and nothing is coming to me.

CHAPTER
Thirty-Four
ROS

Celia is just standing there, glaring at me and as she does, I see her eyes change, like a shutter comes down over her emotions and I know in that moment, she's ready to kill me now. I am afraid, but I won't let Celia see that. I won't give her the satisfaction of it, just like I know no matter how much she's there for Alex after my death, he won't give her the satisfaction of falling for her. At least he'd better not. I don't begrudge him moving on with his life, but if it's with this bitch, I swear I will haunt him. I glare back at her, not showing any fear.

"Goodbye Ros," Celia says, and her hand moves and then suddenly, there's a gun in it and the gun is pointing at me and I know this is it. This is my final moment on earth, and I'm going to die without ever telling Alex I love him.

As if thinking of Alex has conjured him up, there's a sound near the entrance to the office and Celia and I both turn to look, and Alex is standing there just inside the doorway. I wonder if I'm hallucinating, if my fear has fried my brain, but Celia is looking too, standing there with her mouth open in surprise.

Without taking her eyes off Alex, Celia keeps the gun trained on me. I look between the gun and Alex, Alex and the gun. I don't want the gun pointed at me, but I prefer it that way to having this psycho point the gun at Alex. My emotions are cascading crazily between opposites again. I'm so happy to see Alex, to know he has come to save me, but I'm also terrified that he is here because of me and that something bad might happen to him.

Celia takes the safety off the gun, the sound loud in the silence. The gun is still trained on me, and Celia is still watching Alex. I've spotted something else, something I try not to look at too obviously because I don't want to draw Celia's attention to the fact that Will has crept into the room. If anyone can stop this thing without anyone getting hurt, it's Will. This is literally his day job.

"Celia, stop. Put the gun down," Alex says, and my attention goes back to him and then Celia as Celia shakes her head. "I heard what you said Cee. About loving me."

"And?" she demands. "And don't think I'm stupid enough to fall for the whole I love you too, let's be together shit, because I know you're going to try it and I know it's going to be a trap to get the gun off me."

I silently will Alex to be quiet in case he says something that upsets her, but he seems to have a handle on the situation as he tries to talk Celia down.

"I don't think you're stupid for a second," he says. "Hence why I wasn't going to even bother trying that. Here's what I will say, and I mean it one hundred percent. I'm sorry. I'm sorry I didn't notice your feelings for me went beyond friendship, and I'm so sorry I hurt you, even though that was never my intention."

I think Alex genuinely means that. Or I think he would have if this had gone down a different way and Celia didn't have a gun trained on me.

"If you had known, would it have been different?" Celia asks.

I can hear the hope in her voice and in another situation, I would feel sorry for her, but I can't bring myself to even feel pity for her right now.

"Honestly, I don't think it would have been different romantically," Alex tells her, his tone gentle. "But I certainly would have been more aware of your feelings and made sure you weren't having my relationship with Ros put in your face."

"And if you'd never met Ros. What about then? Would there have been a chance for us?" Celia says.

"I can't say for sure Cee, because I don't think anyone knows anything like that for sure. But yeah, maybe there would have been," he says.

Jealousy spikes through me. That had better be a lie. I'm surprised I can feel such a frivolous emotion at this point, but yup, there it is. I force myself to swallow down my jealousy. Alex is actively risking his life trying to save mine. The least I can do is not be mad at him for how he does it. Celia's smiles then and for a moment, she looks genuinely happy, but then the emotion leaves her eyes leaving them blank and empty, and she looks at the gun in her hand, then at me, and then back at Alex.

"So, if she's out of the picture, then maybe one day, you will be mine," she says.

Alex is running before Celia even pulls the trigger, and I try to scream around the gag, knowing it's useless but unable to stop myself as the bang of the shot rings out and Alex falls to the ground with blood coming from him. He lands in a crumpled heap on the floor and immediately, blood begins to pool around him.

As I scream through the gag, producing nothing but a

muffled grunting sound, Will curses and Celia looks at Alex laid in a pool of blood on the ground. Her eyes widen.

"Noooo," she shouts, and for a moment, I think she will go to Alex, but instead, she just stands in place, frozen to the spot, staring at what she has done.

Will looks torn between grabbing her and going to Alex. Alex is dead and beyond help and I should be willing Will to go after that bitch so she can pay for what she's done, but I don't. Instead, I will him to be with Alex, so he isn't laid there alone. Will makes the right choice and crouches down beside Alex as I become aware that I'm sobbing.

Will's movement breaks Celia's spell and she darts away. I'm vaguely aware of Will taking off his t-shirt and pressing it against Alex's stomach and then calling nine one one. I feel like I'm about to pass out, like I'm not really here. But then Will speaks to me, and everything changes again.

"Ros," Will says, his voice penetrating my brain fog. "Ros, listen to me. He's breathing."

The darkness that enshrouded me only moments ago fades away, and hope blossoms light in my chest.

"He's going to be ok," Will confirms. "The ambulance is on its way."

"Ros," I hear Will saying my name from far away as I watch the mind movie of myself learning that Alex isn't dead. "Ros, we're here."

His hand on my arm makes me blink back into reality and I see we're at the hospital. We get out of the car, and I leave the blanket the paramedic gave me behind on the seat and we run to the emergency room entrance. I don't bother going to announce myself at the reception desk, not even when the triage nurse manning it calls after me. I just take off down the corridor, shouting Alex's name. Will runs behind me and grabs my arm.

"Ros, stop," he says.

"I have to see him, Will," I say.

"I know," he says. "But just calm down, ok. He needs you to be calm and normal."

That's about the only thing Will could have said that would have made me calm down a bit, and it's just in time as the triage nurse storms angrily toward us. I know how we must look. Me freaking out screaming for Alex and Will shirtless and covered in blood. It must look as though we attacked someone and we're here to finish the job.

"I'm sorry," I say. "My boyfriend was just shot in front of me, and I need to see him. We followed the ambulance here. His name is Alex. Alex Waters."

Her face softens and she nods her head.

"Come with me," she says.

We follow her and I think she's taking us to Alex, but instead, she takes us to a small room with comfortable looking chairs arranged around a low coffee table and a full coffee machine sitting on a counter behind the seating area, with mugs, sugar and a carton of milk and creamer standing beside it. Before I can start to protest, the triage nurse speaks.

"Alex has been taken straight to the OR. I will get one of the doctors who assessed him to come and talk to you," she says. "Help yourself to coffee."

She leaves the room and Will and I just stand there for a moment and then I half collapse into a chair. I watch Will moving around, not really registering what he's doing until he sits down on the next chair to mine and gives me a cup of coffee. I take it and sip it without really registering that I'm doing it, and the strong taste pulls me back to reality.

"Will he be ok?" I ask.

"Of course he will. He's tougher than you think," Will says.

I don't know if that's true, but I love that Will tells me what I need to hear instead of pussy footing around answering me saying he hopes so, or he's in good hands or some other cliche. I've drunk half of my coffee when the door opens and a man in a white coat comes in.

CHAPTER
Thirty-Five
ROS

"I'm Doctor Flack," he says. "I was the first one to see to Mr. Waters when he came in. I believe you two were present when he was shot?" We both nod, and the doctor goes on. "For the most part, Mr. Waters has been extremely lucky if you can describe someone who has been shot as lucky, in that the bullet didn't hit his kidneys or liver. It did however take a chunk of intestine out hence the reason he's in surgery. It's really nothing, a few stitches and some blood can't solve and because he got here so quickly, I'm hopeful he will make a full recovery."

I feel my whole-body slump at the doctor's words as relief floods me. If I had been standing up, I'm almost certain my knees would have buckled, and I'd be on the ground right now.

Doctor Flack is looking at me with a concerned expression.

"May I take a look at you?" he asks. "You've got a nasty gash there on your head."

"It's nothing," I say.

"Let me be the judge of that," Doctor Flack says with a smile. "You might have a concussion."

"It's fine," I say again, shaking my head. "I want to be here when Alex wakes up."

"And you will be," Doctor Flack says. "This will take five minutes."

Reluctantly, I agree to let the doctor examine me and he takes me out of the room and to a curtained off cubicle. He asks me to sit on the bed and he shines a light into each of my eyes. He smiles at me.

"That's fine," he says. "No sign of any concussion. Now, let me get a nurse in to clean out and treat that wound."

I don't have the energy to argue with him and as long as I'm done when Alex is, I don't much care what they do to me. Doctor Flack leaves the cubicle and I hear him talking to someone outside of the curtain. He explains what happened to me and then the curtain opens and closes again with a whoosh sound and a nurse smiles at me.

"I'm Sasha," she says. "I'm going to clean and treat that wound for you."

She goes to the small sink in the corner and washes her hands and then she opens up the cabinet above it and takes out a kidney bowl, some cotton balls, a small brown bottle of what I believe is iodine, and a roll of band aid material along with a small pair of scissors.

She comes back over and takes the lid off the bottle and dabs some of the liquid inside on the cotton ball and then gently rubs it over the wound. It stings, but not much and it's over quickly. Once she's done that, she cuts the band aid material into strips and holds the wound closed and then sticks them in place.

"All done," she says with a smile, and I thank her and get off the bed.

I go back to the room where Will is waiting.

"No concussion," I tell him. "Just these little strips I could have done myself."

"It's best to be sure," Will says.

"Oh," I say, realizing what's different about Will. He's wearing a navy-blue t-shirt. "You found a t-shirt."

"I bought it from the gift shop of all places," Will says. "Imagine that. Have some grapes, some chocolates, oh, and this t-shirt."

We both laugh and then a silence descends on us. By the time Alex's surgeon comes to the room, we have made and drank three more cups of coffee each. When the surgeon comes in, I don't bother to wait for him to introduce himself.

"Is Alex ok?" I ask.

"He's fine," the surgeon says with a smile. "He's out of recovery and he's in his room. We'll keep him here for a few days of observation, but if you can call anyone who has just been shot lucky, then I would say Alex is indeed lucky."

That's the second person to say that and for the second time I bite my tongue because I know they mean well, but I don't think what happened to Alex is lucky at all.

"Can we see him?" I ask.

"Just for a little while because he needs his rest," the surgeon says.

A little while is better than the no I was expecting to get, and I jump to my feet energized at the thought of seeing Alex and follow the surgeon. He leads us down the corridor and opens a door and gestures for us to enter. I see Alex laid in the bed there, a hospital gown around his shoulders and a blue-colored blanket drawn up to his chest. He turns his head as the door opens, and he smiles when he sees us. I smile back and tears fill my eyes as I practically run to his side.

"I thought I'd lost you," I say.

"It'll take more than that crazy cow to get rid of me," Alex says.

Will brings a chair over from a small stack in the corner and puts it down for me. I thank him and sit down and take

Alex's hand in mine. Alex asks Will to put the bed head up so he can be sitting up and Will obliges and then he stands at the end of Alex's bed.

"When you're well enough, you are in a shit ton of trouble," Will says.

"I figured as much," Alex says with a grin.

Will's cell phone rings and he looks at it and then puts it back in his pocket and grins.

"You're not in as much trouble as Celia is. That was one of my team. She's been arrested and charged with assault, kidnapping and attempted murder," Will says.

I don't like to cheer at someone else's misery, but I am so glad to hear that and judging by the look on Alex's face, he is too.

"I knew Celia was a bitch, but I didn't think she was an actual psycho," I say, shaking my head.

"No. She hid it really well," Alex agrees. "God until today, I would have said she was one of the more level-headed people I knew."

Will nods his agreement. I wouldn't go quite that far, but I know what they mean. Even I, who really didn't like her, didn't think she had a screw loose.

"I'll give you two a few minutes alone," Will says. "I'll be in the corridor whenever you're ready to be taken for your car Ros."

"Thank you," I say.

Will leaves the room and I turn toward Alex and smile at him.

"I thought you were dead, you know. When she shot you," I say. Alex's grip on my hand tightens and I squeeze back. "And the only thought that kept going through my mind was that I hesitated telling you I love you. So here goes. Alex, I love you with all my heart."

"I love you too, Ros," he says. "More than I can ever

explain."

I stand up and lean over and kiss him. He kisses me back, but I feel him wince beneath my lips and I pull away.

"I don't care if it hurts," Alex says.

"Well, I do," I tell him, sitting back down. "We have our whole lives ahead of us for kissing. Right now, you need to concentrate on getting better."

"Listen Ros, I need to ask you something," Alex says. He winces again as he straightens up and kicks his legs off of the bed so he's sitting on the side facing me. "I won't get down on one knee if it's all the same to you, but I love you Ros and I want to spend forever with you. Will you marry me?"

"Yes," I scream. "Oh my God, yes. Of course I will marry you."

I jump up and hug him, being as gentle as I can be.

"I do have a ring," he says, when we finish hugging. "But Celia helped me choose it and I want no part of her in our relationship, so I'm going to get you a different one. Maybe I'll ask Jenny to help."

"Maybe we could choose it together," I suggest.

"Yes, I'd like that," Alex says. "You know, I've been trying to think of the perfect place to propose. I've had a few ideas, but none felt right. I did come up with the worst place though when Celia suggested the place where we shared our first kiss which was of course the office. And here we are. I have officially topped that by proposing in a hospital."

"It was perfect," I say, and I mean it. "Just knowing you want me to be your wife is enough. It doesn't matter where we were when you asked, I would have said yes, and it would have been perfect."

I can see by Alex's face that he's in pain and I stand up again and help him back into bed. He lays back and smiles at me and I sit on the bed beside him.

"Are you going to turn into a major bridezilla now?" he asks.

"God no," I say. "I'm not one for all that stuff. I'd happily do it just me and you, but Fi would never forgive me and I'm sure you want your family there. But I'm thinking small and intimate and a short engagement."

"That sounds like heaven," Alex says.

His eyes start to close. He opens them again but I can see it's taking him a lot of effort to stay awake and so I get up and I kiss his cheek.

"I should go and let you get some rest," I say. I know I was right about how tired he must be when he doesn't argue the point. "I'll see you tomorrow though."

"And the day after that, and the day after that, and the day after that for eternity," Alex mumbles before his eyes close again and stay closed this time. I smile down at him.

My fiancé. My soon to be husband. My life.

Epilogue
ALEX

Three Months Later

We've had our wedding and our honeymoon, and we're back at home. Tomorrow, it's back to work and back to reality, and I still can't actually believe that we are officially married. I mean how on earth did I get so lucky as to have someone like Ros agree to marry me and actually go through with it.

"There he is," Ros says from beside me, nodding toward the door of the restaurant as Will comes in.

I stand up and wave and he comes over and sits down. I wait until he gets settled and then I call our waiter over and order a bottle of champagne. I pour three glasses of it out once it arrives and I hold mine in the air.

"Cheers," I say.

"Cheers," Will and Ros say.

Will and I gulp down a swallow of champagne while Ros sips hers. She always says she doesn't like drinking in the afternoon because it goes to her head, and she quickly switches back to water as Will and I finish our glasses of champagne.

"What's the occasion then?" Will asks.

"I just wanted to thank you again for coming out of retirement to be my best man at my wedding," I say.

A couple of days after I got out of hospital, Will came to me to give me his resignation as my bodyguard. He recommended one of his team to step up and I've been pleased with his performance. Will decided he was ready for something a bit less stressful than keeping me, or anyone else alive, and he chose to become a martial arts instructor.

"I retired as your bodyguard, not your friend," Will says.

"Good because if I get my way, it won't be long until I'm asking you to be the godfather to our first child," I say.

"Consider it a yes already," Will says.

"I hope you actually mean that Will," Ros says. She smiles and rubs her belly. "Because it might be sooner than you think."

"Wait," I say. "Are you telling us you're pregnant?"

Ros nods and grins and I let out a whoop sound without caring that we're in a restaurant.

"Can we get some more champagne please," I call over to our waiter. "I'm going to be a dad."

Some of the initial elation wears off and the enormity of it hits me.

"Shit. I'm going to be a dad. What if I'm awful at it," I say.

"You won't be," Ros says.

"No chance, because you've got Ros to keep you in line," Will laughs.

I spend the rest of the afternoon with a smile on my face and by the end of the meal, I can feel my cheeks aching, but I have never been so happy. I have my perfect woman, my perfect life, and now, the start of my perfect family and I couldn't be happier than I am now. I guess I should call my grandad and thank him for that stupid clause after all.

And they lived happily ever after!

Coming Soon...

IT'S ONLY MAKE-BELIEVE

Prologue
Tia

I take one final glance at the now empty dorm room behind me. All that remains are two empty desks, two chairs and two stripped beds. The posters are gone, the personal effects, the laptops and everything that made the dorm room ours. I look at Louisa and give her a sad smile.

"I can't believe it's over," I say.

"I know," she replies. "It's the end of an era. Four years sharing a room, and we didn't want to kill each other once."

"That in itself feels like more of an achievement than our degrees," I joke.

Louisa laughs and nods in agreement. She links her hand through my arm, careful not to dislodge the box I'm carrying. All of Louisa's stuff is already packed into the trunk of her car and this is the last of mine, the rest of it has also been put away in the trunk of my own car.

"Let's grab lunch before we go," Louisa says, and I nod my agreement gratefully.

I know I have to leave campus, and I know I should be excited to start the rest of my life, but I'm not. Unlike Louisa, who has a family to go home to, I have nothing. My mom died when I was in my first year of college and I'm an only child. Her parents died long ago, and my dad has never been a part of my life. The only thing that man gave me is a surname, something I would have been just as happy to get from my mom. I feel kind of lost now that my final year of college is over if I'm honest, and although having lunch with Louisa will only add an extra hour or so to my time here, I'm still glad for the reprieve.

We walk to my car so I can put my last box in the trunk and then we head to the student canteen where I order a cheeseburger and fries with a soda and Louisa gets a chilli dog with fries and a carton of juice. We pay for our food and find a table and begin eating.

"Do we have to be all grown up now and stop eating junk food after today," I say, trying to keep the mood light.

Louisa snorts out a laugh. "I hope not," she says.

We lapse back into silence, a comfortable silence, the kind that only true friends or soulmates can experience without feeling awkward.

"So, what now?" Louisa asks me after a few more bites of her chilli dog and a small handful of fries.

We've had this conversation several times leading up to the end of the year and I have always bluffed my way through it saying I haven't decided yet, or I have a few options I'm considering. For the first time, I tell her the sad truth.

"I have no idea," I say. "I mean I guess I'll stay here in New York. I have a hotel booked for tonight and I'll have to try and find an apartment and a job."

"You don't have anything lined up?" Louisa asks and I shake my head. "So why stay here in a city you no longer love? You have no one here anymore."

"Thanks for the reminder," I say.

"I didn't mean it like that. I meant come to Chicago. It's way cheaper to get an apartment there than here and there are tons of internships in IT," she says. "You can stay with us until you can rent an apartment."

I think about it for a moment. I have stayed with the Sanchez family a few times in the holidays, and they are lovely, welcoming people and I love staying with them. But if I do this, I will have to find an apartment quickly. I don't want them to think I'm taking their kindness for granted. Do I want this though? I think for a moment longer and I realize that I can't think of a single reason not to do it. I grin at Louisa.

"OK. Chicago it is," I say.

"Correct answer. But first, let's take advantage of that hotel room you have booked and have one last night in New York," Louisa says with a grin, and I nod, my own grin spreading across my face as I feel a weight lifting from my shoulders.

Chapter One
Luke

I walk away from my car, where it's parked in my reserved parking space, and I head to the entrance of the headquarters of Sold, an online auction website that I am the CEO of. I started Sold at just the right time and it took off more than I had ever even dared to dream it would, and the company is now worth over a billion dollars.

I enter the lobby and the receptionist greets me. I return the greeting and head to the elevator. The first five floors of the building belong to Sold and I ride up to the fifth floor where my office is. The lobby and elevator car are busy as it's that time of the morning where the majority of people are coming in to work. I greet and am greeted by some employees and a few people from other firms who I'm now on speaking terms with after seeing them around the building so often.

The elevator pings to a stop on the fifth floor and I get out of it and head along the hallway to my office.

"Morning Mel," I say as I duck my head around my PA's door. "Any messages?"

"Morning," Mel replies. "Only one important one. Enrique Sanchez called. He requested you call him back. He said it's urgent."

"Thanks Mel," I say, and I continue on to my office, wondering what Enrique might want that is so urgent.

Enrique Sanchez is the highest shareholder in Sold after me and he's the chairman of the board of directors. He very rarely interferes in the day to day running of the business, and it's unusual for him to call me like this out of the blue.

I get to my office, go inside and take my jacket off. I take my cell phone from the pocket and then hang it on one of the coat hooks on the wall behind my door. I move across my spacious office and sit down behind the large oak desk. I fire up my computer out of habit because usually my first task is checking the stock value of the company, but today, my first task is calling Enrique back.

I scroll through my cell phone and find his number which I type into my office phone. I put my cell phone in my top drawer while I listen to the ringing sound down my ear. I don't have long to wait before Enrique answers my call with a gruff hello.

"Enrique? Hi, it's Luke Jackson returning your call," I say.

"Ah. Good morning, Luke. How are you?" he asks. His words carry the slightest hint of his Spanish accent, but he speaks English as well as anyone I've ever met.

"I'm good thanks. How are you?" I ask.

His voice is giving nothing away as to the reason for his call, although he doesn't sound pissed off, so I guess that's a good thing.

"I'll be better in a moment if you agree to do me a small personal favor," he says.

"Go on," I say.

I'm not stupid enough to agree to the favor before I know what it is, but I will certainly hear him out, and if it's something I can do, I will do it. Enrique holds a lot of sway when it comes to company votes and a lot of the smaller shareholders just vote whichever way he does, so it's always a good idea to keep him on my side.

"I need you to give my daughter, Louisa, an internship," Enrique says.

My heart sinks at his words. When he said a personal favor, I thought maybe he wanted to borrow my driver for a few days, or something like that. Not something that involves the company. I want to help Enrique, but I won't let the company carry dead weight. My employees have enough to do at the moment, especially now that Diane has left the web development team, and the last thing the staff needs is to have to babysit Enrique's daughter. He must sense some of my thoughts from my silence, because he goes on before I get a chance to say no.

"Although I'm asking as a favor, Louisa is qualified. She's just graduated from NYU with a degree in web development and she has an offer from a tech company here, but one of the conditions of employment is that she has three months experience," Enrique says.

That definitely changes things slightly and I find myself agreeing to take Louisa on. She sounds like she will help the web development team rather than get in the way and it's a nice solution to our short staff problem. It also means I have three months to find a permanent replacement for Diane instead of having to rush into taking the first person who fits the bill.

"I won't ask my daughter to do something I wouldn't do myself, so the internship can't be unpaid," Enrique says to me. "But I understand from a business standpoint that the company needs to do that. I will pay Louisa a wage, but she needs to be under the impression it comes from the company. She knows better than to discuss salary with other employees so it's not like anyone will know."

"Ok," I agree.

"And lastly. Don't treat her like my daughter. Treat her like any other intern. Louisa is a bright girl, and I'm confident she can do anything you ask of her, but she's … er…. lazy is the wrong word. Unmotivated I think is maybe better," Enrique says. "I hate to use the word spoiled or entitled, but she seems to think she can lie about the experience needed and the company won't find out. Honestly, I don't think she cares much if they do. She seems to think she can coast through life on my dime and it's time for her to see that's not going to wash anymore."

He might not like the words spoiled or entitled, but it doesn't change the fact that based on the description he has just given me, his daughter is definitely one of those things. Maybe even both.

"So, you're sending me a lazy, entitled girl who technically doesn't need a job. Thanks for that," I say, half joking. "I'm sure she'll be a valuable asset."

Enrique laughs.

"Something like that. But as I said, she's a bright girl and I have no doubt that underneath that spoiled exterior, there's a woman who can make it in this field or any other field she chooses. I think she just needs to experience the real world a little bit more, you know, where she is answerable to someone other than her mom and me and is expected to perform just like everyone else," Enrique says.

"Don't worry," I say. "I'll kick her ass and make her employable."

"That's what I wanted to hear. Thanks Luke. I owe you one. I'll tell her she starts at nine am sharp on Monday morning," Enrique says.

I agree and he hangs up. I replace the receiver and sit for a moment. I hope I can keep the promise I've just made, because having Enrique owe me one is exactly what I need right now, because I have a big idea that I'm working on and it will be ready to pitch to the board by the end of the year, and I really want Enrique's support on it.

Chapter Two
Tia

Louisa stands up as I walk across the bar towards her. I reach the table, and we hug.

"I'm so sorry I'm late," I say as we sit down. "Honestly, I know like two people in Chicago, and I'm late to meet one of them because the other one called, and I lost track of time."

Louisa wrinkles her nose.

"You're not seriously considering getting back with Justin, are you?" Louisa asks.

I shake my head.

"No. As a couple we just didn't work, there was no chemistry between us. But we got along well enough and there's no harm in being friends. And besides, in a brand new city, I'm hardly in a place to turn my back on someone I actually know," I tell her.

"I still think it's creepy that he followed you here," Louisa says.

I roll my eyes.

"For the fiftieth time, he didn't follow me here. He took a job offer here before he even knew I was coming here. Hell, it was before I had even decided to come here," I say.

"That's what he tells you," Louisa says. "But is it the truth?"

I roll my eyes again and Louisa takes the hint and laughs and pushes a glass of rose wine towards me.

"Forget Justin, drink up," she says.

I pick up the glass and take a big sip and moan my appreciation when the cold sweetness of the wine runs over my tongue. I swallow my first mouthful and take another drink.

"You look like you needed that," Louisa says.

"I did," I agree. "Job hunting is thirsty work. Especially when there are so few options. I mean don't get me wrong, there are tons of jobs I could do, but I don't want to stack shelves or fold clothes. I want something actually related to my degree. There's just nothing. Well, there are unpaid internships of course but I need money. I'm starting to think I'm going to have to take an unpaid internship and then wait tables or tend bar or something on evenings and weekends."

"Funny you should say that" Louisa says. "I actually have something I thought you might be interested in."

I feel my interest being piqued and I sit up straighter and look at Louisa, waiting for her to go on. I'm struck, certainly not for the first time, and probably not for the last time, how pretty Louisa is. She has caramel crème colored skin with dark brown eyes and dark brown curls. She has a lovely, curvaceous figure, and she is as beautiful inside as she is outside. I still sometimes have to pinch myself to believe that she chose me, Tia Lake, a self-confessed nobody, to be her best friend at college and now beyond.

"Earth calling," Louisa says, and I snap back to attention.

"Sorry," I say. "I was miles away."

Louisa laughs.

"Yeah, I saw," she says. "I was just saying not to get too excited about the proposal I have for you. It's paid work, but it's only an internship so the pay isn't fantastic, but …"

"But it'll give me experience that will give me a chance at getting a foot in the door somewhere," I finish for her. "And might mean I don't have to work a second job too."

"Exactly," Louisa agrees. "So, you're interested then?"

I nod.

"Yes," I say. "Let me just go and grab us some more drinks and then I want to hear all about it."

I get up and head for the bar before Louisa can object. It's no secret that I'm not exactly drowning in money. In fact, I have enough in my bank account for like two months of rent and bills and when that's gone, I have nothing. Louisa on the other hand comes from money and while her father is getting a bit pissed off with her not working by all accounts, she still isn't going to be homeless or have to choose between heating and food any time soon. For that reason, Louisa is more than happy to pay on nights out, but I like to be able to pay my way. I love Louisa and I know her offer comes from a place of her love for me, but I want to be on equal footing, not her little charity case that she drags out when she needs an excuse to feel good about herself. I know that's not fair, but it's how I feel, and I can't help it.

I get served with two Aperol Spritz cocktails and go back to the table. I set one down in front of Louisa and she nods her head in approval.

"Nice," she says after a sip. "So, this internship. It's with a big tech company and it will be mostly working with the web development team from what I understand about it, although obviously it's an internship so you'll probably have to do some dog's body work as well."

"Yeah, I would expect that," I agree. "What's the catch."

"Who said there was going to be a catch?" Louisa says. Her innocent look only convinces me that there's a catch and that it's a big one. I don't answer and she sighs. "Fine. There is a catch. But it's a teeny tiny one. You have to pretend to be me."

I look at gorgeous, Latina Louisa and then down at myself. I'm the picture someone would paint if they were asked to draw a person who was the opposite to Louisa. Firstly, I am so white, milk feels sorry for me. My hair is a light blonde, a natural shade that almost no one believes is natural, and my eyes are bright blue. Where Louisa is short and curvy, I'm tall and willowy. I definitely got my mom's Scandinavian looks.

"Who the hell is going to believe I am you?" I say.

"No one at the company has seen me," Louisa says. "There's no reason why they won't. And this way, we both win. You will get paid for doing the sort of thing you want to do, and I will get my father off my back because he will think I'm doing the internship. And the reference at the end can easily be used by both of us, we just need to make a copy and change the name."

I can feel myself on the verge of saying yes, although it still feels like I'm not getting the whole story.

"It pays eight hundred dollars a week after deductions," Louisa says.

"Ok. I'm in," I say.

Fuck the catch. That will pay for my rent which is almost fifteen hundred dollars a month – a bargain for a one-bedroom apartment in downtown Chicago I am assured by

Louisa – and leave me with enough left over for utilities, food, and maybe even a bit of a social life.

"Congratulations on the new job," Louisa grins. "You start at nine o'clock on Monday morning. I'll text you the address and the details. I'd say don't be late, but you're meant to be me, so feel free."

She laughs and I roll my eyes and laugh with her. When we stop laughing, Louisa goes to the bar and this time, we're drinking something called a Mellow Marshmallow. It's sweet and a bit coconutty and I like it. While she was gone, a question came to my mind. I'm about to ask it, although I'm not sure I really want to know the answer.

"Louisa, I have to ask. This internship. It's paid which is practically unheard of. Even the odd paid internship I've heard of pays closer to six hundred dollars a week and this is eight hundred dollars after deductions. Is there something I should know?" I ask.

"Well, now that you mention it, there was something about disposing of dead bodies, but it's only now and again, and you probably won't have to do more than one or two," Louisa says with a grin.

I laugh and shake my head, and she turns serious again and shrugs one shoulder.

"I assume they are paying a bit more than average because they think it's actually going to be me and my dad is on the board of directors," Louisa says.

My mouth drops open. I think I would have preferred the first explanation. There's no way I can take this job now. It explains why Louisa was careful not to mention the name of the company. I didn't notice at the time, but I do now. If she had mentioned it was Sold sooner, it would have been an instant no from me. I have already purposely avoided looking for any positions at the company after learning Enrique is on the board because I didn't want it to come out that I knew his daughter, and have it look like that's why I got the job. Now, she's suggesting I should pretend to be her there. How could that ever work?

"I'm out," I say. "You told me no one at the company knew what you looked like. I think your dad might know your face. And he knows me too."

"That's the beauty of it. He and my mom leave tomorrow for a cruise around Europe. The internship will be done by the time they return. My dad will hear how wonderful I was, because obviously it's you and you rock, and you will have some high powered job by then," Louisa says.

"I don't know," I say, looking down into my almost empty glass.

"Look at it this way. You pretending to be me isn't a crime. The worst thing that can happen if it does come out, is my dad will be pissed at me, which he is right now anyway and you'll get fired, meaning you won't have a job, which you don't right now anyway. See what I mean? In the worst case scenario, things go back to how they are right now, that's it. And in every other scenario, everything gets one hundred percent better for both of us," Louisa says.

She grins at me, nodding her head ever so slightly as I think. I don't even know why I'm thinking about it. Or at least pretending to be. The money sold me, but I can never say no to Louisa anyway, although this is the first one of her schemes or ideas that I can see seriously backfiring on us. But fuck it. I am actually going to give this a shot.

"Nine o' clock Monday morning. Sold, here I come," I say.

Louisa whoops and then drains her drink and motions for me to do the same. I finish it up and Louisa gets up, pulling me up with her and leading me out of the bar.

"But Monday at nine o'clock is almost thirty six hours away. So, let's go to a club and dance and drink and celebrate your new job."

"That is the best idea you've had in ages," I say with a grin, and I turn towards the road and flag down a passing cab, and we get in it to go to the club.

>Please pre-order here:
>It's Only Make Believe

About the Author

Thank you so much for reading!
If you have enjoyed the book and would like to leave a precious review for me, please kindly do so here:

Surviving The New Boss

Please click on the link below to receive info about my latest releases and giveaways.
<u>NEVER MISS A THING</u>

Or
come say 'hello' here:

Also by Jona Rose

Nanny Wanted

CEO's Secret Baby

New Boss, Old Enemy

Craving The CEO

Forbidden Touch

Crushing On My Doctor

Reckless Entanglement

Untangle My Heart

Tangled With The CEO

Tempted By The CEO

CEO's Assistant

Trouble With The CEO

It's Only Temporary

Charming The Enemy

Keeping Secrets

On His Terms

CEO Grump

Surprise CEO

The Fire Between Us

The Forgotten Pact

Taming The CEO Beast

Hot Professor

Flirting With The CEO

Surprise Proposal

Propositioning The Boss

Dream Crusher

Until He Confesses

Insufferable Boss

Strictly Business

Confessing To The CEO

Enemy Boss

The Bride's Brother

The Bet

One Bossy Night

Not Yet Yours

Made in United States
Orlando, FL
21 January 2025